Counsel
for
Christian
Workers

Counsel for Christian Workers

C. H. Spurgeon

CHRISTIAN FOCUS

Copyright © Christian Focus Publications

ISBN 1-85792-652-8

10 9 8 7 6 5 4 3 2 1

This edition published in 2001
reprinted 2006
in the
Christian Heritage Imprint
by
Christian Focus Publications Ltd.,
Geanies House, Fearn, Ross-shire,
IV20 1TW, Great Britain

www.christianfocus.com

Cover design by Moose77.com

Printed and bound by
Nørhaven Paperback A/S

Contents

You perhaps may have little idea how ...
Mr. Whitfield who preached this sermon which they
showed in their congregation... before, so above
their high steeple, from one generally ... sections of
a certain house with a colonel-hunter for the last sound
he was at once a Christian, to make way ... least with
an hour to ... by the great, and to conquer with the
general ... make with a good ... child ... but his wife
and daughters; that an ... the ... to make, to have better
information ... he would have come ... they can
... a child's character. He had ... he would with
them too, to sleep, anticipated the top with ... the hours
of God and with more ... he ... he ... in ...

These people ... and ... now ... was ... fitted in
... and I have not been helping to them. I could do
no better than I must tell ... why ... whatever good
many they have to they do ... to recover a scene they
are has ... the more are braved.

After prayer she still felt compassion in his spirit.
I loved none more ... "I cannot do ... but the little

I

AN EARNEST MAN

You perhaps may have heard the story of
Mr. Whitefield, who made it his wont wherever he
stayed to talk to the members of the household about
their souls – with each one personally. But stopping at
a certain house with a Colonel, who was all that could
be wished except a Christian, he was so pleased with
the hospitality he received, and so charmed with the
general character of the good Colonel and his wife
and daughters, that he did not like to speak to them
about decision, as he would have done if they had
been less amiable characters. He had stopped with
them for a week, and during the last night, the Spirit
of God visited him so that he could not sleep.

'These people,' said he, 'have been very kind to
me, and I have not been faithful to them; I must do
it before I go; I must tell them that whatever good
thing they have, if they do not believe in Jesus they
are lost.' He arose and prayed.

After praying he still felt contention in his spirit.
His old nature said, ' I cannot do it,' but the Holy

Spirit seemed to say, 'Leave them not without warning.' At last he thought of a device, and prayed God to accept it; he wrote upon a diamond-shaped pane of glass in the window with his ring these words: 'One thing thou lackest.' He could not bring himself to speak to them, but went his way with many a prayer for their conversion.

He had no sooner gone than the good woman of the house, who was a great admirer of him, said, 'I will go up to his room: I like to look at the very place where the man of God has been.' She went up and noticed on the windowpane those words, 'One thing thou lackest.' It struck her with conviction in a moment. 'Ah!' said she, 'I thought he did not care much about us, for I knew he always pleaded with those with whom he stopped, and when I found that he did not do so with us, I thought we had vexed him: but I see how it was; he was too tender in mind to speak to us.'

She called her daughter up. 'Look there, girls!' said she, 'see what Mr Whitefield has written on the window! "One thing thou lackest." Call up your father.' And the father came up and read that too, 'One thing thou lackest!' and around the bed whereon the man of God had slept they all knelt down and sought that God would give them the one thing they lacked, and ere they left that chamber they had found that one thing, and the whole household rejoiced in Jesus.

It is not long ago since I met with a friend, one of whose church members preserves that very pane of glass in her family as an heirloom. Now, if you cannot admonish and warn in one way, do it in another: but take care to clear your soul of the blood of your relatives and friends, so that it may never crimson your skirts and accuse you before God's bar. So live and so speak and teach, by some means or other, that you shall have been faithful to God and faithful to the souls of men.

Earnestness often gives prudence, and puts a man in the possession of tact, if not of talent. Andrew used what ability he had. If he had been as some young men are of my acquaintance, he would have said, 'I should like to serve God. How I should like to preach! And I should require a large congregation.' Well, there is a pulpit in every street in London, there is a most wide and effectual door for preaching in this great city of ours beneath God's blue sky. But this young zealot would rather prefer an easier berth than the open air; and because he is not invited to the largest pulpits, does nothing.

How much better it would be if, like Andrew, he began to use the ability he had among those who are accessible to him, and from that stepped to something else, and from that to something else, advancing year by year! If Andrew had not been the means of converting his brother, the probabilities are that he never would have been an apostle. Christ had some reason in the choice of his apostles to their office, and perhaps the ground of his choice of Andrew as an apostle was this: 'he is an earnest man,' said he, 'he brought me Simon Peter; he is always speaking privately to individuals I will make an apostle of him.'

Young men, if you become diligent in tract distribution, diligent in the Sunday school, you are likely men to be made into ministers; but if you stop and do nothing until you can do every-thing, you will remain useless – an impediment to the church instead of being a help to her. Dear sisters in Jesus Christ, you must none of you dream that you are in a position in which you can do nothing at all. That were such a mistake in providence as God cannot commit. You must have some talent entrusted to you, and something given you to do which no one else can do. Find out, then, what your sphere is, and occupy it. Ask God to tell you what is your niche, and stand in it, occupying the place till Jesus Christ shall come and give you your reward. Use what ability you have, and use it at once.

Andrew proved his wisdom in that he set great store by a single soul. He bent all his efforts at first upon one man. Afterwards, Andrew, through the Holy Spirit, was made useful to scores, but he began with one. What a task for the arithmetician, to value one soul! One soul sets all heaven's bells ringing by its repentance. One sinner that repenteth maketh angels rejoice. What if you spend a whole life pleading and labouring for the conversion of that one child? If you win that pearl it shall pay you your life worth. Be not therefore dull and discouraged because your class declines in numbers, or because the mass of those with whom you labour reject your testimony. If a man could earn but one in a day he might be satisfied. 'One what?' saith one. I meant not one penny, but one thousand pounds. 'Ah,' say you, 'that would be an immense reward.' So if you earn but one soul you must reckon what that one is; it is one for numeration, but for value it exceeds all that earth could show. What would it profit a man if he gained the whole world and lost his soul? and what loss would it be to you, if you did lose all the world, and gained your soul, and God made you useful in the gaining of the souls of others? Be content, and labour in your sphere, even if it be small, and you will be wise.

You may imitate Andrew in *not going far afield to do good*. Many Christians do all the good they can five miles off from their own house, when the time they take to go there and back might be well spent in the vineyard at home. I do not think it would be a wise regulation of the parochial authorities if they required the inhabitants of St. Mary, Newington, to remove the snow from the pavement of St. Pancras, and the inhabitants of St. Pancras to keep clean the pavement of St. Mary, Newington. It is best and most convenient that each householder should sweep before his own door; so it is our duty to do, as believers, all the good we can in the place where God has been pleased to locate us, and especially in our own households.

If every man has a claim upon me, much more my own offspring. If every woman has some demand upon me as to her soul, so far as my ability goes, much more such as are of my own flesh and blood. Piety must begin at home as well as charity. Conversion should begin with those who are nearest to us in ties of relationship. I stir you up, not to be attempting missionary labours for India, not to be casting eyes of pity across to Africa, not to be occupied so much with tears for popish and heathen lands, as for your own children, your own flesh and blood, your own neighbours, your own acquaintance. Lift up your cry to heaven *for them*, and then afterwards you shall preach among the nations. Andrew goes to Cappadocia in his afterlife, but he begins with his brother; and you shall labour where you please in years to come, but first of all your own household, first of all those who are under your own shadow must receive your guardian care. Be wise in this thing; use the ability you have, and use it amongst those who are near at hand.

Perhaps somebody will be saying, 'How did Andrew persuade Simon Peter to come to Christ?' He did so, first, by narrating his own personal experience: he said, 'We have found the Messiah.' What you have experienced of Christ tell to others. He did so next by intelligently explaining to him what it was he had found. He did not say he had found some one who had impressed him, but he knew not who he was; he told him he had found the Messiah, that is, Christ. Be clear in your knowledge of the gospel and your experience of it, and then tell the good news to those whose souls you seek. Andrew had power over Peter because of his own decided conviction. He did not say, 'I hope I have found Christ,' but, 'I have found him.' He was sure of that. Get full assurance of your own salvation. There is no weapon like it. He that speaks doubtingly of what he would convince another, asks that other to doubt his testimony. Be positive in your experience and your assurance, for this will help you.

Andrew had power over Peter because he put the good news before him in an earnest fashion. He did not say to him, as though it were a commonplace fact, 'The Messiah has come,' but no, he communicated it to him as the most weighty of all messages with becoming tones and gestures, I doubt not, 'We have found the Messiah, which is called Christ.' To your own kinsfolk tell your belief, your enjoyments, and your assurance, tell all judiciously, with assurance of the truth of it, and who can tell whether God may not bless your work?

Andrew won a soul, won his brother's soul, won such a treasure! He won no other than that Simon, who at the first cast of the gospel net, when Christ had made him a soul-fisherman, caught three thousand souls at a single haul! Peter, a very prince in the Christian Church, one of the mightiest of the servants of the Lord in all his usefulness, would be a comfort to Andrew. I should not wonder but what Andrew would say in days of doubt and fear, 'Blessed be God that he has made Peter so useful! Blessed be God that ever I spoke to Peter! What I cannot do, Peter will help to do; and while I sit down in my helplessness, I can feel thankful that my dear brother Peter is honoured in bringing souls to Christ.' Your fingers are yet to wake to ecstasy the living lyre of a heart that up till now has not been tuned to the praise of Christ, you are to kindle the fire which shall light up a sacred sacrifice of a consecrated life to Christ. Only be up and doing for the Lord Jesus, be importunate and prayerful, be zealous and self–sacrificing. I make no doubt of it, that, when we have proved our God by prayer, he will pour down such a blessing that we shall not have room to receive it.

2

ANGELS VISIT SODOM

The angels never hesitated when they were bidden to go to Sodom. They descended without demur and went about their work without delay. Although the report of Sodom's detestable iniquity had gone up to heaven, and the Lord would bear no longer with that filthy city, yet, from the purity of heaven, the angels did not hesitate to descend to behold the infamy of Sodom; where God sent them, they failed not to go. 'There came two angels to Sodom at even.' What, *angels*? Did angels come to Sodom? To *Sodom*, and yet angels? Aye, and none the less angelic because they came to Sodom, but all the more so, because in unquestioning obedience to their Master's high behests they sought out the elect one and his family, to deliver him and his from impending destruction. However near to Christ you may be, however much your character may be like that of your Lord, you, who are called to such service, must never say, 'I cannot talk to these people, they are so depraved and debased; I cannot enter that haunt of sin to tell of Jesus; I sicken at the thought;

its associations are altogether too revolting to my feelings;' but, because you are there wanted, men of God, you must there be found.

To whom should the physician go but to the sick, and where can the distributor of the alms of mercy find such a fitting sphere as among those whose spiritual destitution is extreme? Be ye angels of mercy each one of you, and God speed you in your soulsaving work. As ye have received Christ Jesus into your hearts, so imitate him in your lives. Let the woman that is a sinner receive of your kindness, for Jesus looked on her with mercy; let the man who has been most mad with wickedness be sought after, for Jesus healed demoniacs; let no type of sin, however terrible, be thought by you to be beneath your pity, or beyond your labour, but seek ye out those who have wandered farthest, and snatch from the flame the firebrands which are already smoking in it.

When you go to lost souls, you must, as these angels did, tell them plainly their condition and their danger. 'Up,' said they, 'for God will destroy this place.' If you really long to save men's souls, you must tell them a great deal of disagreeable truth. The preaching of the wrath of God has come to be sneered at nowadays, and even good people are half-ashamed of it, a maudlin sentimentality about love and goodness has hushed, in great measure, plain gospel expostulations and warnings. But, if we expect souls to be saved, we must declare unflinchingly with all affectionate fidelity, the terrors of the Lord.

'Well,' said the Scotch lad, when he listened to the minister who told his congregation that there was no hell, or at any rate only a temporary punishment, 'Well,' said he, 'I need not come and hear this man any longer, for if it be as he says, it is all right, and religion is of no consequence, and if it be not as he says, then I must not hear him again, because he will deceive me.'

'Therefore,' says the apostle, 'knowing the terrors of the Lord we persuade men.' Let not modern squeamishness prevent plain speaking. Are we to be more gentle than the apostles? Shall we be wiser than the inspired preachers of the Word? Until we feel our minds overshadowed with the dread thought of the sinner's doom we are not in a fit frame for preaching to the unconverted. We shall never persuade men if we are afraid to speak of the judgment and the condemnation of the unrighteous. None so infinitely gracious as our Lord Jesus Christ, yet no preacher ever uttered more faithful words of thunder than he did. It was he who spoke of the place 'where their worm dieth not and their fire is not quenched.' It was he who said, 'These shall go away into everlasting punishment.' It was he who spake the parable concerning that man in hell who longed for a drop of water to cool his tongue. We must be as plain as Christ was, as downright in honesty to the souls of men, or we may be called to account for our treachery at the last. If we flatter our fellows into fond dreams as to the littleness of future punishment, they will eternally detest us for so deluding them, and in the world of woe they will invoke perpetual curses upon us for having prophesied smooth things, and having withheld from them the awful truth.

Where words suffice not, as they frequently will not, you must adopt other modes of pressure. The angel took them by the hand. I have much faith under God in close dealings with men; personal entreaties, by the power of the Holy Spirit, do wonders. To grasp a man's hand while you speak with him may be wise and helpful, for sometimes, if you can get one by the hand and show your anxiety by pleading with him, God will bless it. It is well to cast your words, as men drop pebbles into a well, right down into the depth of the soul, quietly, solemnly, when the man is alone. Often is such a means effectual where the preacher with his sermon has laboured in vain.

If you cannot win men by words, you must say to yourself, 'What can I do?' and go to the Lord with the same inquiry. By the pertinacity of your earnestness you must trouble them into thoughtfulness. As by continual coming the woman wearied the unjust judge, so do you by your continual anxiety and perseverance weary them in their sins, till they will fain give you a little heed, in order, if possible, to be rid of you, if for nothing else. If you cannot reach them because they wilt not read the Bible, yet you can thrust a good book in their way, which may say to them what you cannot say; you can write them a letter, short but earnest, and tell them how you feel; you can continue in prayer for them; you can stir up the arm of God, and beseech the Most High to come to the rescue.

There have been cases in which, when everything else has failed, a tear, a tear of disappointed love, has done the work. I think it was Mr. Knill who, one day, when distributing tracts amongst the soldiers, was met by a man who cursed him, and said to his fellowsoldiers, 'Make a ring round him, and I will stop his tract distributing once for all,' and then he uttered such fearful oaths and curses that Knill, who could not escape, burst into a flood of tears. Years afterwards, when he was preaching in the streets, a grenadier came up, and said, 'Mr. Knill, do you know me?' 'No, I do not,' said he, 'I don't know that I ever saw you.' 'Do you recollect the soldier who said, 'Make a ring round him and stop his tract distributing,' and do you recollect what you did?' 'No, I do not.' 'Why, you broke into tears, and when I got home those tears melted my heart, for I saw you were so in earnest, that I felt ashamed of myself, and now I preach myself that same Jesus whom once I despised.' Oh, that you might have such a strong love for perishing sinners that you will put up with their rebuffs and rebukes, and say to them, 'Strike me if you will, but hear me; ridicule me, but still I will plead with you; cast me under your feet as though I were the offscouring of all things, but at any rate, I will not let you perish, if it be in my power to warn you of your danger.'

3

Workers Who Are Successful

'How is it likely,' says one, 'that we can hope to make an impression upon the present age? What means have we but the simple gospel of Jesus Christ?' We are certainly not among the wealthy, and we count not amongst us the great ones of the land. Our membership has always been, and still is, among the poor. How shall we expect to tell upon so huge a city as this, or to exert any influence upon so great a country; and, above all, how shall we make any impress upon the population of the whole globe? We are weak, but we are not weaker than the first disciples of Christ. Neither were they learned, nor were they the wealthy, of the earth: fishermen, the most of them, by no means men of cultivated ability – their tramp was that of a legion that went forth to conquer as well as to fight. Wherever they went and wielded the sword of the Spirit, which is the Word of God, their enemies were put to confusion. It is true they died in the conflict. Some of them were slain by the sword, and others of them were rent in sunder by wild beasts; but in all these things they were more than conquerors through him that loved them.

The primitive church did tell upon its age and left a seed behind which the whole earth could not destroy; and so shall we by God's grace if we are equally set upon it, equally filled with the divine life, equally resolved by any means and by all means to spread abroad the savour of Jesus Christ's name; our weakness shall be our strength, for God shall make it to be the platform upon which the omnipotence of his grace shall be displayed. Keep together, keep close to Christ; close up your ranks. Heed the battle cry; hold fast the faith; quit yourselves like men in the conflict, and the gates of hell shall not prevail against you. Only may the King himself lead us onward to the fray, and we shall not fear the result.

If we pant to see the Word of God increase, multitudes added to the disciples, and a great company of those who are least likely to be saved brought in, there must be an adequate instrumentality. Nothing can avail without the operation of the Holy Spirit and the smile from heaven. Paul planteth, Apollos watereth, and God giveth the increase. We must never begin our catalogue of outward means without referring to that blessed and mysterious potentate who abides in the church, and without whom nothing is good, nothing efficient, nothing successful.

'Come, Holy Spirit, heavenly dove,
With all thy quickening powers.'

This should be our first prayer whenever we attempt to serve God, for if not, we begin with pride, and can little hope to succeed by prowess. If we go to the warfare at our own charges we must not marvel if we return stained with defeat. Oh Spirit of the living God, if it were not for thy power we could not make the attempt, but when we rely upon thee we go forward in confidence!

I have been struck lately, in looking through the history of the Reformation and of the times before the Reformation, with the remarkable downrightness of the testimony of the early preachers. If you look at the life of Farel you find him not preaching *about* the gospel, but preaching *the gospel*. So it was with John Calvin. He is looked upon now, of course, as a theologian only, but he was really one of the greatest of gospel preachers. When Calvin opened the Book and took a text, you might be sure that he was about to preach 'Through grace are ye saved, and that not of yourselves, it is the gift of God.' And it was the same with Luther. Luther's preaching was just the ringing of a big bell, the note of which was always, 'Believe on the Lord Jesus Christ and live! It is not of works, lest any man should boast, but by faith are ye saved, and by faith alone.' They spake this, and they spake it again; neither did they couch the doctrine in difficult words, but they laboured with all their might, so to speak, that the ploughman at the ploughtail should understand, and that the fishwife should comprehend the truth. They did not aim at lofty periods and flowing eloquence; of rhetoric they had a most contemptible opinion, but they just dashed right on with this one truth.

He that believeth hath everlasting life: 'Believe on the Lord Jesus Christ, and thou shalt be saved.' If we are to see the church of God really restored to her pristine glory, we must have back this plain, simple, gospel preaching. I do believe that the hiding of the cross beneath the veil of fine language and learned dissertation is half the cause of the spiritual destitution of our country. Jesus Christ came into the world to save sinners.

We must have not only plain preaching but plain teaching. Sunday school teachers must teach this same gospel. A certain denomination has made the confession that after having had their schoolrooms crowded with children, they do not know that any of those children have afterwards come to be attendants at the places of worship. Miserable confession! Miserable teachers must they be! And have we not known teachers who believed in the doctrines of grace, and they would have fought earnestly for them, but in the schoolroom they have twaddled to the little children in this kind of way 'Be good boys and girls; keep the Sabbath; do not buy sweets on a Sunday;

mind your fathers and your mothers; be good, and you will go to heaven!'–which is not true, and is not the gospel; for the same gospel is for little children as for grownup men – not 'Do this and live,' which is after the law that was given by Moses, but 'Believe and live,' which is according to the grace and truth that came by Jesus Christ. Teachers must inculcate the gospel if they are to see the salvation of their classes; the gospel, the whole gospel, and nothing but the gospel, for without this no great thing will be done.

And if we would see the gospel spread abroad here as once it did in Geneva, as once, under John Knox, it did in Scotland, as it did in Luther's day throughout Germany, we must have much holy living to back it all up. After we have done the sermon, people say, 'How about the people that attend there? What about the church-members, are they upright? Are they such people as you can trust? What about their homes? Do they make good husbands? Are they good servants? Are they kind masters?' People will be sure to inquire this, and if the report of our character be bad, it is all over with our testimony. The doctor may advertise, but if the patients are not cured, he is not likely to establish himself as being well skilled in his art; and the preacher may preach, but if his people do not love the gospel, they kick down with their feet what he builds up with his hands.

Yet all this would not suffice unless we add individual personal exertion. According to Christ's law, every Christian is to be a minister in his own sphere; every member of the church is to be active in spreading the faith which was delivered not to the ministers, but delivered to the saints, to every one of them, that they might maintain it and spread it according to the gift which the Spirit has given them.

Shall I venture a parable? A certain band of men, like knights, had been exceedingly victorious in all their conflicts. They were men of valour and of indomitable courage; they had carried everything before them, and subdued province after province for their king. But on a sudden they said in the council chamber, 'We have at our head a most valiant warrior, one whose arm is stout enough to smite down fifty of his adversaries; would it not be better if, with a few such as he to go out to the fight, the mere men-at-arms, who make up the ordinary ranks, were to stop at home? We should be much more at our ease; our horses would not so often be covered with foam, nor our armour be bruised in returning from the fray, and no doubt great things would be done.' Now, the foremost champions, with fear and trembling, undertook the task and went to the conflict, and they fought well, no one could doubt it; to the best of their ability they unhorsed their foe and they did great exploits.

But still, from the very hour in which that scheme was planned and carried out, no city was taken, no province was conquered, and they met together and said, 'How is this? Our former prestige is forgotten; our ranks are broken; our pennons are trailed in the dust; what is the cause of it?' When out spoke the champion, and said, 'Of course it is so! How did you think that some twelve or fifteen of us could do the work of all the thousands? When you all went to the fight, and every man took his share, we dashed upon the foe like an avalanche, and crushed him beneath our tramp; but now that you stay at home and put us, but a handful, to do all the work, how can you expect that great things should be done?'

So each man resolved to put on his helmet and his armour once again, and go to the battle, and so victory returned. We must not spare a single one, neither man nor woman, old nor young, rich nor poor, but you must each fight for the Lord Jesus according to your ability, and that his kingdom may come, and that his will may be done upon earth even as it is in heaven.

4

GIANTS AND DWARFS

It is needful, whenever any holy enterprise is commenced, that it should be early watered by the helpful Spirit of God. Nothing beginneth well unless it beginneth in God. It cannot take root, it cannot spring up in hopefulness, except the Holy Spirit shall descend upon it; it will wither like the grass upon the housetops if the celestial dew of the morning fall not early upon it. The like grace is equally needful after years of growth; there is urgent need of the latter rain, the shower of revival, in which the old work shall be freshened, and the first verdure shall be restored; for without this latter rain, the period of harvest, which is the end aimed at, will be disappointing.

The same is true in connection with any sphere of labour in which any individual may happen to be engaged. I will trust that every believer has found something to do for his Lord and Master. In commencing any Christian work, novelty greatly assists enthusiasm, and it is very natural that under first impulses the beginner should achieve an easy success. The difficulty of the Christian is very seldom the commence-ment of the work; the true labour lies in the perseverance which alone can win the victory. Christians who have now been for years occupied with a service which the Holy Ghost laid upon them, I would remind of the early rain of their youthful labours, the moisture of which still lingereth on their memories, although it has been succeeded by long years of drought.

Be encouraged; a latter rain is yet possible. Seek it. That ye need it so much is a cause for sorrow, but if you really feel your need of it, be glad that the Lord worketh in you such sacred desires. If you did not feel a need for more grace, it would be a reason for alarm; but to be conscious that all that God did by you in the past has not qualified you to do anything without him now, to feel that you lean entirely upon his strength now as much as ever, is to be in a condition in which it shall be right and proper for God to bless you abundantly. Wait upon him, then, for the latter rain; ask that if he has given you a little of blessing in past years, he would return and give you ten times as much now, even now; so that, at the last, if you have sown in tears, you may come again rejoicing, bringing your sheaves with you.

Alas; the danger of every Christian worker is that of falling into routine and self-sufficiency. We are most apt to do what we have been accustomed to do, and to do it half asleep. One of the hardest tasks in all the world is to keep the Christian awake on the Enchanted Ground. The tendencies of this present time, and of all times, are soporific. The life, the power of our public services and private devotion speedily evaporates; we pray as in a dream, and praise and preach like somnambulists. May God be pleased to stir us up, to awaken and quicken us, by sending us the latter rain to refresh his weary heritage.

We have in this age but few giants in grace who rise head and shoulders above the common height, men to lead us on in deeds of heroism and efforts of unstaggering faith. After all, the work of the Christian church, though it must be done by all, often owes its being done to single individuals of remarkable grace. In this degenerate time we are very much as Israel was in the days of the Judges, for there are raised up among us leaders who judge Israel, and are the terror of her foes. Oh, if the church had in her midst a race of heroes; if our missionary operations could be attended with the holy chivalry which marked the church in the early days; if we could have back apostles and martyrs, or even such as Carey and Judson, what wonders would be wrought! We have fallen upon a race of dwarfs, and are content, to a great extent, to have it so.

The fact is, the most of us are vastly inferior to the early Christians, who, as I take it, were persecuted because they were thoroughly Christians, and we are not persecuted because we hardly are Christians at all. They were so earnest in the propagation of the Redeemer's kingdom, that they became the nuisance of the age in which they lived. They would not let errors alone. They had not conceived the opinion that they were to hold the truth, and leave other people to hold error without trying to intrude their opinions upon them, but they preached Christ Jesus right and left, and delivered their testimony against every sin. They denounced the idols, and cried out against superstition, until the world, fearful of being turned upside down, demanded of them, 'Is that what you mean? Then we will burn you, lock you up in prison, and exterminate you.'

To which the church replied, 'We will accept the challenge, and will not depart from our resolve to conquer the world for Christ.'

At last the fire in the Christian church burned out the persecution of an ungodly world.

But we are so gentle and quiet, we do not use strong language about other people's opinions; but let men go to hell out of charity to them. We are not at all fanatical, and for all we do to disturb him, the old manslayer has a very comfortable time of it. We would not wish to save any sinner who does not particularly wish to be saved. We shall be pleased to say a word to them in a mild way, but we do not speak with tears streaming down our cheeks, groaning and agonizing with God for them; neither would we thrust our opinions upon them, though we know they are being lost for want of the knowledge of Christ crucified. May God send the latter rain to his church, to me, and to you, and may we begin to bestir ourselves, and seek after the highest form of earnestness for the kingdom of King Jesus. May the days come in which we shall no longer have to complain that we sow much and reap little, but may we receive a hundredfold reward, through the grace of our Lord Jesus Christ!

Very feebly, but still with the most earnest intentions, I have endeavoured to excite in you an ambition after a higher life, and the setting up of a higher standard. Seek to love your Master more; pray to be filled with his Spirit. Do not be mere tradespeople who are Christianized, but be Christians everywhere; not plated goods, but solid metal. Be ye servants of Jesus Christ, whether ye eat or drink, or whatsoever ye do. Serve him with both your hands, and all your heart. Get your manhood strung to the utmost tension, and throw its whole force into your Redeemer's service. Live while you live. Drivel not away your existence upon baser ends, but count the glory of Christ to be the only object worthy of your manhood's strength, the spread of the truth the only pursuit worthy of your mental powers. Spend and be spent in your Master's service.

5

OBEDIENCE

The path of obedience is generally a middle path. 'Turn not from it, to the right hand nor to the left.'

There is sure to be a right hand, there is sure to be a left hand, and both are probably wrong. There will be extremes on either side. I believe that this is true in ten thousand things in ordinary life, and also true in spiritual things in very many respects.

The path of truth in doctrine is generally a middle one. There are certain tremendous truths, such as divine sovereignty, the doctrine of election, covenant transactions, and so forth; and some men cast such a loving eye upon these truths that they desire to be, and are, quite blind to all other truths besides. These great and precious doctrines take up the whole field of their vision, and another and equally valuable part of God's Word is either left unread, or else twisted round into some supposed reconciliation with the first-named truths.

Then again, there are others who think much of man. They have deep sympathy with the human race. They see man's sin and ruin, and they are much charmed with the mercy of God, and the invitations of the gospel which are given to sinners, and they become so entranced with these truths in connection with the responsibility of man, and man's free agency, that they will see nothing else, and declare all other doctrines, except these, to be delusions. If they admit the doctrines of grace to be true, they think them valueless, but they generally consider them to be untrue altogether. It seems to me that the path of truth is to believe them both; to hold firmly that salvation is by grace, and to hold with equal firmness that the ruin of any man is wholly and entirely his own fault; to maintain the sovereignty of God, and to hold the responsibility of man also; to believe in the free agency of both God and man; neither to dishonour God by making him a lackey to his creatures' will, nor, on the other hand, to rid man of all responsibility, by making him to be a mere log or a machine. Take all that is in the Bible to be true. Never be afraid of any text that is written by the sacred pen. When you turn the pages over, I do hope you never feel as if you wish that any verse could be altered, I trust you never desire that any text might be amended so as to read a little more Calvinistic, or a little more like the teaching of Arminius. Always stand to it that your creed must bend to the Bible, and not the Bible to your creed, and dare to be a little inconsistent with yourselves, if need be, sooner than be inconsistent with God's revealed truth.

With regard to our words, the course of speech generally is, on the one hand to say too much, or on the other hand to say too little; to be silent when the wicked are before us, or else to be rash with our lips and betray a good cause through our rashness in defending it. There is a time to speak, and there is a time to be silent, and he that judgeth well will mark his opportunities and take the middle course. He will neither be garrulous with advice that is not required, nor will he be cowardly and dumb when he ought to bear testimony for his Master. The same holds good with regard to zeal.

Neither to the right hand nor to the left must the Christian turn, with regard to the reliance of his soul, in the matter of his eternal salvation. 'None but Jesus' must be the constant watchword of our spirit. Some will call us in this direction, and some in that. The wrecker's beacons would entice us upon the rocks in a thousand directions, but let us steer by the sun or by the polestar, and not trust to the treacherous guides of human fancy. Keep close to this, that 'other foundation can no man lay than that which is laid, Jesus Christ the righteous.'

So in *the matter of faith itself*, let us keep the middle place. Let us not be as some are, presumptuous, and refusing to examine themselves, declaring that they must be right. Let us remember that

'He who never doubted of his state,
He may – perhaps he may too late.'

Let us not fall, on the other side, into constant doubting, imagining that we never can be fully assured, but must always be raising the question:

> 'Tis a point I long to know,
> Oft it causes anxious thought;
> Do I love the Lord or no?
> Am I his, or am I not?'

Let us ask God to guide us into the middle path, wherein we can say, 'I know whom I have believed, and am persuaded that he is able to keep that which I have committed unto him until that day'; careful, watchful, prayerful, as much as if our salvation depended upon our own vigilance; relying upon the sure promise, and the immutable oath, knowing that we stand in Christ, and not in ourselves, and are kept by the mighty God of Jacob, and not by any power of our own. This middle path, wherein we turn not to the right hand of presumption, nor to the left hand of unbelief, is the path which God would have us tread.

This rule, too, for I might continue to apply it in scores of ways, will *also hold good with you in your daily life in the matter of your general cheerfulness or otherwise*. Some people never smile. Dear souls! They pull the blinds down on Sunday. They are sorry that the flowers are so beautiful, and think that they ought to have been whitewashed; they almost believe that if the garden beds were of a little more serious colour it would be advisable.

Let no man be deceived with the idea that if he carries out the right, by God's grace he will prosper in this world as the consequence. It is very likely that, for a time at least, his conscientiousness will stand in the way of his prosperity. God does not invariably make the doing of the right to be the means of pecuniary gain to us. On the contrary, it frequently happens that for a time men are great losers by their obedience to Christ. But the Scripture always speaks as to the long run; it sums up the whole of life – there it promises true riches.

If thou wouldst prosper, keep close to the Word of God, and to thy conscience, and thou shalt have the best prosperity. Thou wilt not see it in a week, nor a month, nor a year, but thou shalt enjoy it ere long. Hundreds have I seen, and I speak within bounds when I speak of that number, who in different times of dilemma have waited upon me, and asked my advice as to what they should do. I have almost always noticed that those persons who temporize, or attempt to find out a policy of going between, and doing as little wrong as possible, but still just a little, always blunder out of one ditch into another, and their whole life is a life of compromises, of sins, and of miseries; if they do get to heaven they go there slipshod, and with thorns piercing their feet all the way.

But I have noticed others who have come right straight out, and rent away the cords which entangled them, and they have said, 'I will do the right, if I die for it'; and though they have had to suffer (I could mention some cases where they have suffered for years, very much to the sorrow of him who gave them the advice upon which they acted, not because he regretted giving them the advice, but regretted that they had to suffer), yet always there has been a turn somewhere or other, and by and by they have had to say, 'I thank God, after all, notwith-standing all my crosses and losses, that I was led to be faithful to my convictions, for I am a happier man, if not a richer man.' In some cases they have absolutely been richer men, for after all, even in this world, 'honesty *is* the best policy.' It is a very low way of looking at it, but right and righteousness do in the end, in the long run, get the respect and the esteem of men. The thief, though he takes a short way to get rich, yet takes such a dangerous way that it does not pay; but he who walks straight along the narrow road shall find it to be the shortest way to the best kind of prosperity, both in this world and in that which is to come.

One good brother, whose shoe latchet I am not worthy to unloose, said, on one occasion, that when he went up the Rhine, he never looked at the rocks, or the old castles, or the flowing river, he was so taken up with other things! Why, to me, nature is a looking-glass in which I see the face of God. I delight to gaze abroad, and

'Look through nature up to nature's God.'

But that was all unholiness to him. I confess I do not understand that kind of thing; I have no sympathy with those who look upon this material world as though it were a very wicked place, and as if there were here no trace whatever of the divine hand, and no proofs of the divine wisdom, nor manifestations of the divine care. I think we may delight ourselves in the works of God, and find much pleasure therein, and get much advanced towards God himself by considering his works. That to which I have thus referred is one extreme. There are others who are all froth and levity, who profess to be Christians, and yet cannot live without the same amusements as worldlings; must be now at this party, and then at that; never comfortable unless they are making jokes, and following after all the levities and frivolities of the world. Ah! the first is a pardonable weakness, in which there is much that is commendable, but this is a detestable one, of which I can say nothing that is good. The Christian, I think, should steer between the two. He should be cheerful, but not frivolous. He should be sustained and happy under all circumstances; have a friendly and a kindly word for all, and be a man among men as the Saviour was, willing to sit at the banquet, and to feast and rejoice with those that do rejoice; but still heavenly-minded in it all, feeling that a joy in which he cannot have Christ with him is no joy, and that places of amusement where he cannot take his Lord with him are no places of amusement, but scenes of misery to him. He should be constantly cheerful, happy, and rejoicing, and yet at the same time he should evince a deep solemnity of spirit which removes far from him everything that is sacrilegiously light and trifling.

By the same rule, *arrange your business*. Some men in business act in such a way that from morning till night they can think of nothing but business. I have had to mourn over some Christians who, when they have had enough, did not know it – when they were doing as much as they could do with health to their souls, and had no more need of gain, yet they must needs launch out into something else that would take away all opportunities of serving God's cause, and all time for reflection and thought, and that would thus bring barrenness and leanness into their souls. Others we have to complain of, who do not work enough at their callings. They are at a sermon when they ought to be behind the counter, or they are enjoying a prayer meeting when they ought to be mending their husband's stockings. They go out preaching in the villages when they had better be earning money to pay their creditors. There are extremes; but the true Christian is diligent in business, and is also fervent in spirit, seeking to combine the two. The believer would be like one of old, 'a just man and devout,' not having one duty smeared with the blood of another duty.

6

'ONLY BE THOU STRONG AND VERY COURAGEOUS'

(Joshua 1:7)

'Only be thou strong and very courageous, that thou
mayest observe to do according to all the law, which
Moses my servant commanded thee.' You supposed
when you heard the words, 'Only be thou strong and
very courageous,' that some great exploit was to be
performed, and the supposition was correct, for all
exploits are comprehended in that one declaration,
'That thou mayest observe to do according to all the
law, which Moses my servant commanded thee.' The
highest exploit of the Christian life is to obey Christ.
This is such an exploit as shall never be performed
by any man, except he has learned the rule of faith,
has been led to rest upon Christ, and to advance upon
the path of obedience in a strength which is not his
own, but which he has received from the work of the
indwelling Holy Ghost. The world counts obedience
to be a mean-spirited thing, and speaks of rebellion as
freedom. We have heard men say, 'I will be my own

master; I shall follow my own will.' To be a freethinker and a freeliver seems to be the worldling's glory, and yet if the world could but have sense enough to convict itself of folly, upon indisputable proof being afforded it, it were not difficult to prove that a reviler of the obedient is a fool. Take the world's own martial rule. Who is accounted to be the boldest and the best soldier but the man who is most thoroughly obedient to the captain's command?

There is a story told of the old French wars which has been repeated hundreds of times. A sentinel is set to keep a certain position, and at nightfall, as he is pacing to and fro, the emperor himself comes by. He does not know the password. Straightway the soldier stops him. 'You cannot pass,' says he. 'But I must pass,' says the emperor. 'No,' replies the man, 'if you were the little corporal in gray himself you should not go by,' by which, of course, he meant the emperor. Thus the autocrat himself was held in check by order. The vigilant soldier was afterwards handsomely rewarded, and all the world said that he was a brave fellow. Now, from that instance, and there are hundreds of such which are always told with approbation, we learn that obedience to superior commands, carried out at all hazards, is one of the highest proofs of courage that a man can possibly give; to this the world itself gives its assent. Then surely it is not a mean and sneaking thing for a man to be obedient to him who is the Commander-in-chief of the universe, the King of kings, and Lord of lords. He who would do the right and the true thing in cold blood in the teeth of ridicule, is a bolder man than he who flings himself before the cannon's mouth for fame; aye, and let me add, to persist in scrupulous obedience throughout life may need more courage than even the martyr evinces when once for all he gives himself to burn at the stake.

In Joshua's case, full obedience to the divine command involved innumerable difficulties. The command to him was, that he should conquer the whole of the land for the favoured tribes, and to the best of his ability he did it; but he had to besiege cities which were walled up to heaven, and to fight with monarchs whose warriors came to battle in chariots of iron, armed with scythes. The first conflicts were something terrible. If he had not been a bold and able soldier, he would have put up his sword and desisted from the strife; but the spirit of obedience sustained him. Though you and I have no Hivites and Jebusites to kill, no cities to pull down, no chariots of iron to encounter, yet we shall find it no easy thing to keep to the path of Christian consistency.

Moreover, Joshua had not only difficulties to meet with, but he made a great many enemies through his obedience. This was naturally so. As soon as it was known that Jericho had been taken, that Ai had been carried by assault, then we read of first one confederation of kings and then of another, their object being to destroy the power of Joshua, since these kings well knew that he would crush them if they did not crush him. Now, the Christian man is in a like plight. He will be sure to make enemies. It will be one of his objects to make none; but, on the other hand, if to do the right, and to believe the true, and to carry out the honest, should make him lose every earthly friend, he will count it but a small loss, since his great Friend in heaven will be yet more friendly and reveal himself to him more graciously than ever.

Joshua, in his obedience, needed much courage, because he had undertaken a task which involved, if he carried it out, long years of perseverance. After he had captured one city, he must go on to attack the next fortress. The days were not long enough for his battles. He bids the sun stand still, and the moon is stayed; and even when that long day has passed, yet the morning sees him sword in hand still. Joshua was like one of those old knights who slept in their armour. He was always fighting. His sword must have been well hacked, and often must his armour have been blood red. He had before him a lifelong enterprise. Such is the life of the Christian, a warfare from end to end. As soon as you are washed in Christ's blood and clothed in his righteousness, you must begin to hew your way through a lane of enemies, right up to the eternal throne. Every foot of the way will be disputed; not an inch will Satan yield to you. You must continue daily to fight. 'He that endureth to the end, the same shall be saved;' not the beginner who commences in his own strength, and soon comes to an end, but he who, girt about with divine grace, with the Spirit of God within him, determines to hold on till he has smitten the last foe, and never leaves the battlefield till he has heard the word, 'Well done, good and faithful servant!' Let the man who says that the Christian's life is mean, and devoid of manliness, let him go and learn wisdom before he speaketh; for of all men the persevering believer is the most manly. Thou who boastest of thyself, of thy courage in sinning, thou yieldest to the foe; thou art a cringing cur; thou turnest tail upon the enemy; thou courtest the friendship of the world; thou hast not courage enough to dare to do the right and the true; thou hast passed under the yoke of Satan and thine own passions, and to conceal thine own cowardice thou art base enough to call the brave Christian man a coward. Out on thee, for adding lying to thine other vices!

Oftentimes, if we follow Christ we shall need to be brave indeed in facing the world's customs. You will find it so, young man, in a mercantile house. You will find it so, husband, even in connection with your own wife and children, if they are unsaved. Children have found this so in the school. Traders find it so in the market place. He that would be a true Christian had need wear a stout heart.

There is a story told of Dr. Adam Clarke, which shows the courage which the youthful Christian sometimes needs. When he was in a shop in the town of Coleraine, they were preparing for the annual fair, and some rolls of cloth were being measured. One of them was too short, and the master said, 'Come, Adam, you take that end, and I will take the other, and we will soon pull it, and stretch it till it is long enough.' But Adam had no hands to do it with, and no ears to hear his master's dishonest order, and at last he flatly refused, whereupon the master said, 'You will never make a tradesman; you are good for nothing here; you had better go home, and take to something else.'

Now, that thing may not be done now, for men do not generally cheat in that open, downright kind of way nowadays, but they cheat after more roguish fashions. The records of the Bankruptcy Court will tell you what I mean. Bankruptcies one after another of the same person are double-distilled thieving, generally; not old-fashioned thieving like that which once brought men to transportation and to the gallows, but something worse than highway robbery and burglary.

The genuine Christian will every now and then have to put his foot down, and say, ' No, I cannot, and I will not be mixed up with such a thing as that,' and will have to say this to his master, to his father, to his friend, whose respect he desires to gain, and who may be of the greatest possible assistance to him in life. But if it be your duty, my dear brother and sister, thus to do the right, do it if the skies fall. Do it if poverty should stare you in the face. Do it if you should be turned into the streets tomorrow. You shall never be a loser by God in the long run; and if you have to suffer for righteousness' sake, blessed are you!

Count yourselves to be happy that you have the privilege of making any sacrifice for the sake of conscience, for in these days we have not the power to honour God as they did who went to prison, and to the rack, and to the stake; let us not, therefore, cast aside other opportunities which are given to us of showing how much we love the Lord, and how faithfully we desire to serve him. Be very courageous to do what the Lord Jesus bids you in all things, and let men judge you to be an idiot if they will, you shall be one of the Lord's champions, a true knight of the Cross.

The world saith, 'We must not be too precise.' Hypocritical world! The world means that it would be glad to get rid of God's law altogether, but as it scarcely dares to say that point-blank, it cants with the most sickening of all cant, 'We must not be too particular, or too nice.' As one said to an old Puritan once, 'Many people have rent their consciences in halves: could not you just make a little nick in yours?' ' No,' he said, 'I cannot, for my conscience belongs to God.' 'We must live, you know,' said a money-loving shopkeeper, as his excuse for doing what he could not otherwise defend. 'Yes, but we must die,' was the reply, 'and therefore we must do no such thing.' There is no particular necessity for any of us living. We are probably better dead, if we cannot live without doing wrong.

The very essence of obedience, I have said, lies in exactness. Probably your child, if some times disobedient, would still, as a general rule, do what you told him. It would be in the little things that thoroughgoing and commendable obedience would appear. Let the world judge of this for itself. Here is an honest man. Do people say of him, 'He is such an honest man that he would not steal a horse?' No, that would not prove him to be very honest; but they say, 'He would not even take a pin that did not belong to him.' That is the world's own description of honesty, and surely when it comes to obedience to God it ought to be the same. Here is a merchant, and he boasts, ' I have a clerk, who is such a good accountant that you would not find a mistake of a single penny in six months' reckoning.' It would not have meant much if he had said, 'You would not find a mistake of ten thousand pounds in six months' reckoning.' And yet if a man stands to little things, and is minute and particular, worldlings charge him with being too stringent, too strict, too straight-faced, and I know not what besides; while all the time, according to their own showing, the essence of honesty and of correctness is exactness in little things.

7

THE KIND OF LABOURERS WANTED

What kind of men does the Master mean to use?
They must be *labourers*.

The man who does not make hard work of his
ministry will find it very hard work to answer for his
idleness at the last great day. A gentleman who wants
an easy life should never think of occupying the
Christian pulpit, he is out of place there, and when
he gets there the only advice I can give him is to get
out of it as soon as possible; and if he will not leave
the position voluntarily, I call to mind the language of
Jehu concerning Jezebel, 'Fling her down,' and think
the advice applicable to a lazy minister. An idler has
no right in the pulpit. He is an instrument of Satan
in damning the souls of men. The ministry demands
brain labour; the preacher must throw his thought into
his teaching, and read and study to keep his mind in
good trim. He must not weary the people by telling
them the truth in a stale, unprofitable manner, with
nothing fresh from his own soul to give force to it.
Above all, he must put heart work into his preaching.

He must feel what he preaches: it must never be with him an easy thing to deliver a sermon, he must feel as if he could preach his very life away ere the sermon is done. There must be soul work in it, the entire man must be stirred up to effort, the whole nature that God has endowed him with must be concentrated with all its vigour upon the work in hand. Such men we want. To stand and drone out a sermon in a kind of articulate snoring to a people who are somewhere between awake and asleep must be wretched work. I wonder what kind of excuse will be given by some men at last for having habitually done this. To promulgate a dry creed, and go over certain doctrines, and expound and enforce them logically, but never to deal with men's consciences, never to upbraid them for their sins, never to tell them of their danger, never to invite them to a Saviour with tears and entreaties! What a powerless work is this! What will become of such preachers? God have mercy upon them! We want labourers, not loiterers. We need men on fire, and I beseech you ask God to send them. The harvest never can be reaped by men who will not labour; they must off with their coats and go at it in their shirtsleeves; I mean they must doff their dignities and get to Christ's work as if they meant it, like real harvest men. They must sweat at their work, for nothing in the harvest field can be done without the sweat of the face, nor in the pulpit without the sweat of the soul.

But what kind of labourers are required? They must be *men who will go down into the wheat*. You cannot reap wheat by standing a dozen yards off and beckoning to it: you must go up close to the standing stalks; every reaper knows that. And you cannot move people's hearts, and bring men to Christ, by imagining yourself to be a superior being who condescends wonderfully when he shakes hands with a poor man. There is a very genteel order of preaching which is as ridiculous as reaping with a lady's ivory-handled pocket knife, with kid gloves on; and I do not believe in God's ever blessing it. Get among the wheat, like men in earnest! God's servants ought to feel that they are one with the people; whoever they are they should love them, claim kinship with them, feel glad to see them, and look them in the face and say, Brother. Every man is a brother of mine; he may be a very bad one, but for all that I love him, and long to bring him to Jesus. Christ's reapers must get among the wheat.

Now, see what the labourer brings with him. It is a sickle. His communications with the corn are sharp and cutting. *He cuts right through*, cuts the corn down, and casts it on the ground. The man whom God means to be a labourer in his harvest must not come with soft and delicate words, and flattering doctrines concerning the dignity of human nature, and the excellence of self-help, and of earnest endeavours to rectify our lapsed condition, and the like. Such mealy-mouthedness may God curse, for it is the curse of this age. The honest preacher calls a sin a sin, and a spade a spade, and says to men, 'You are ruining yourselves; while you reject Christ you are living on the borders of hell, and ere long you will be lost to all eternity. There shall be no mincing the matter, you must escape from the wrath to come by faith in Jesus, or be driven forever from God's presence, and from all hope of joy.' The preacher must make his sermons cut. He is not to file off the edge of his scythe for fear it should hurt somebody. The gospel is intended to wound the conscience, and to go right through the heart, with the design of separating the soul from sin and self, as the corn is divided from the soil. Our object is to cut the sinner right down, for all the comeliness of the flesh must be slain, all his glory, all his excellence must be withered, and the man must be as one dead ere he can be saved. Ministers who do not aim to cut deep are not worth their salt. God never sent the man who never troubles men's consciences. Such a man may be an ass treading down the corn, but a reaper he certainly is not. We want faithful ministers; pray God to send them.

But then a labourer has only begun when he cuts the corn: much more is wanted. As he cuts, he lets the corn fall on to his arm, and then he lays it along in rows, but afterwards *he binds it together* and makes it into bundles that it may be ingathered. So the labourer whom God sends into the field must be a gathering labourer; he must be one who brings God's people together, who comforts those that mourn, and picks up from the earth those who were cut down by the sharp sickle of conviction. He must bind the saints together, edifying them in their most holy faith.

Remember also that the labourer's work is never done in harvest time till he sees the corn housed – until it is made into a stack or put into a barn, his toil is not over; and the Christian minister, if God has truly anointed him to his work, never leaves caring for souls till they get to heaven. He is like Mr. Greatheart, with Christiana and Mercy and the children; he goes with them from the City of Destruction, right up to the River Jordan; and if he could he would go through the river with them. It is his business to march in front with his shield to meet the dragons and giants with his sword, and protect the little ones. It is his to be tender to them as a shepherd with the lambs and a nurse with her children, for he longs to present them at the last to his Master and say, 'Here am I, and the children that thou hast given me.'

We are to pray *to the Lord*, for it is the Lord's business. Only the Lord can send us the right men. He has a right to send whom he pleases, for it is his own harvest, and a man may employ whom he wills in his own field. It would be all in vain to appeal to anybody else. It is of no use to appeal to bishops to find us labourers. God alone has the making of ministers, and the raising up of true workers, and therefore the petition must be addressed to him. 'Pray ye therefore the Lord of the harvest.' The Lord's prayer, in its first three petitions, contains this prayer: 'Our Father which art in heaven, hallowed be thy name. Thy kingdom come, thy will be done, in earth, as it is in heaven.' Does not that mean, 'Lord, send forth men who may teach this world to hallow thy name, that they through thy Spirit's power may be the means of making thy kingdom come, and causing thy will to be done in earth as it is in heaven.' We ought to pray continually to the great Lord of the harvest for a supply of earnest labourers.

And do you notice the expression used here, 'that he would *send forth* labourers'? Now, the Greek is much more forcible, it is that he would push them forward, and thrust them out; it is the same word which is used for the expulsion of a devil from a man possessed. It takes great power to drive a devil out, it will need equal power from God to drive a minister out to his work. I always say to young fellows who consult me about the ministry, 'Don't be a minister if you can help it;' because, if the man can help it, God never called him, but if he cannot help it, and he must preach or die, then he is the man. May the Lord push men out, thrust them out, drive them out, and compel them to preach the gospel; for unless they preach by a divine compulsion, there will be no spiritual compulsion in their ministry upon the hearts of others. 'Pray ye therefore the Lord of the harvest, that he would thrust out labourers into his harvest.'

8

A Young Convert and Successful Worker

It has very frequently happened that while men have been sketching out imaginary designs, they have missed actual opportunities. They would not build because they could not erect a palace; they therefore shiver in the winter cold. They would not be clothed in homespun, for they looked for scarlet and fine linen ere long; they were not content to do a little, and therefore did nothing. It is vain for us to be praying for an extensive revival of religion, and comforting each other in the hope of it, if meanwhile we suffer our zeal to effervesce, and sparkle, and then to be dissipated. Our proper plan is, with the highest expectations, and with the largest longings, to imitate the woman of whom it is written, 'She hath done what she could,' by labouring diligently in such holy works as may be within our reach, according to Solomon's precept, 'Whatsoever thy hand findeth to do, do it with thy might.' While believers are zealously doing what God enables them to do, they are in the high road to abundant success; but if they stand all the day idle, gaping after wonders, their spiritual want shall come upon them as an armed man.

Andrew was earnest for the souls of others, though he was but a young convert. He appears to have beheld Jesus as the Lamb of God one day, and to have found out his brother Peter the next. Far be it from us to forbid you who but yesterday found joy and peace, to exert your newborn zeal and youthful ardour. No, delay not, but make haste to spread abroad the good news which is now so fresh and so full of joy to you. It is right that the advanced and the experienced should be left to deal with the captious and the skeptical, but you, even you, young as you are, may find some with whom you can cope: some brother like Simon Peter, some sister dear to you, who will listen to your unvarnished tale, and believe in your simple testimony.

Andrew was a disciple, a new disciple, a commonplace disciple, a man of average capacity. He was not at all the brilliant character that Simon Peter his brother turned out to be. Throughout the life of Jesus Christ Andrew's name occurs, but no notable incident is connected therewith. Though in after life he no doubt became a most useful apostle, and according to tradition sealed his life's ministry by death upon a cross, yet at the first Andrew was, as to talent, an ordinary believer, one of that common standard and nothing remarkable. Yet Andrew became a useful minister, and thus it is clear that servants of Jesus Christ are not to excuse themselves from endeavouring to extend the boundaries of his kingdom by saying, 'I have no remarkable talent, nor singular ability.'

I very much disagree with those who decry ministers of slender gifts, sneering at them, as though they ought not to occupy the pulpit at all. Are we, after all, as servants of God, to be measured by mere oratorical ability ? Is this after the fashion of Paul, when he renounced the wisdom of words lest the faith of the disciples should stand in the wisdom of man, and not in the power of God? If you could blot out from the Christian church all the minor stars, and leave nothing but those of the first magnitude, the darkness of this poor world would be increased seven fold. How often the eminent preachers, which are the church's delight, are brought into the church by those of less degree, even as Simon Peter was converted by Andrew! Who shall tell what might have become of Simon Peter if it had not been for Andrew? Who shall say that the church would ever have possessed a Peter if she had closed the mouth of Andrew? And who shall put their finger upon the brother or sister of inferior talent and say, 'These must hold their peace'? Nay, if thou hast but one talent, the more zealously use it. God will require it of thee: let not thy brethren hold thee back from putting it out to interest. If thou art but as a glowworm's lamp, hide not thy light, for there is an eye predestinated to see by thy light, a heart ordained to find comfort by thy faint gleam. Shine thou, and the Lord accept thee.

Every single professor of the faith of Christ is bound to do something for the extension of the Redeemer's kingdom. I would that all, whatever their talents, would be like Andrew in promptness. He is no sooner a convert than he is a missionary; no sooner taught than he begins to teach. I would have them like Andrew, *persevering*, as well as prompt. He first finds Peter – that is his first success, but how many afterwards he found, who shall tell? Throughout a long life of usefulness it is probable that Andrew brought many stray sheep to the Redeemer's fold, yet certainly that first one would be amongst the dearest to his heart. 'He first findeth Peter:' he was the spiritual father of many sons, but he rejoiced most that he was the father of his own brother Peter – his brother in the flesh, but his son in Christ Jesus.

The object of the soulwinner is not to bring men to an outward religiousness merely. Little will you have done for a man if you merely make the Sabbath-breaker into a Sabbath-keeper, and leave him a self-righteous Pharisee. Little will you have done for him if you persuade him, having been prayerless, to be a mere user of a form of prayer, his heart not being in it. You do but change the form of sin in which the man lives; you prevent him being drowned in the salt water, but you throw him into the fresh; you take one poison from him, but you expose him to another. The fact is, if you would do real service to Christ, your prayer and your zeal must follow the person who has become the object of your attention, till you bring him absolutely to close with grace and lay hold on Jesus Christ, and accept eternal life as it is found in the atoning sacrifice. Anything short of this may have its usefulness for this world, but must be useless for the world to come.

9

'WITH GOOD WILL DOING GOOD SERVICE'
(Ephesians 6:7)

Our great Captain would not have you hope to win the victory by leaving your post. He would have you abide in your trade, calling or profession, and all the while serve the Lord in it, doing the will of God from the heart in common things. This is the practical beauty of our holy faith, that when it casts the devil out of a man it sends him home to bless his friends by telling them how great things the Lord has done for him. Grace does not transplant the tree, but bids it overshadow the old house at home as before, and bring forth good fruit where it is.

Grace does not make us unearthly, though it makes us unworldly. True religion distinguishes us from others, even as our Lord Jesus was separate from sinners, but it does not shut us up or hedge us round about as if we were too good or too tender for the rough usage of everyday life. It does not put us in the saltbox and shut the lid down, but it casts us in among our fellowmen for their good. Grace makes us the servants of God while still we are the servants of men: it enables us to do the business of heaven while we are attending to the business of earth: it sanctifies the common duties of life by showing us how to perform them in the light of heaven.

The love of Christ makes the lowliest acts sublime. As the sunlight brightens a landscape and sheds beauty over the commonest scene, so does the presence of the Lord Jesus. The spirit of consecration renders the offices of domestic servitude as sublime as the worship which is presented upon the sea of glass before the eternal throne by spirits to whom the courts of heaven are their familiar home.

Whether we are servants or masters, whether we are poor or rich, let us take this as our watch-word, '*As to the Lord, and not to men.*' Henceforth may this be the engraving of our seal and the motto of our coat-of-arms; the constant rule of our life and the sum of our motive. In advocating this gracious aim of our being, let me say that if we are enabled to adopt this motto it will, first of all, influence our work itself; and, secondly, it will elevate our spirit concerning that work. Yet let me add that if the Lord shall really be the all-in-all of our lives, it is after all only what he has a right to expect, and what we are under a thousand obligations to give to him.

If we do indeed live 'as to the Lord,' we must needs live wholly to the Lord. The Lord Jesus is a most engrossing Master. He has said, 'No man can serve two masters,' and we shall find it so. He will have everything or nothing. If, indeed, he be our Lord, he must be sole Sovereign, for he will not brook a rival. It comes to pass, then, Christian, that you are bound to live for Jesus and for him alone. You must have no coordinate or even secondary object or divided aim; if you do divide your heart, your life will be a failure. As no dog can follow two hares at one time, or he will lose both, certainly no man can follow two contrary objects and hope to secure either of them. No, it behoves a servant of Christ to be a concentrated man: his affections should be bound up into one affection, and that affection should not be set on things on the earth, but on things above; his heart must not be divided, or it will be said of him as of those in Hosea, 'Their heart is divided; now shall they be found wanting.' The chamber of the heart is far too narrow to accommodate the King of kings and the world, or the flesh, or the devil, at the same time.

What a mean and beggarly thing it is for a man only to do his work well when he is watched. Such oversight is for boys at school and mere hirelings. You never think of watching noble-spirited men. Here is a young apprentice set to copy a picture: his master stands over him and looks over each line, for the young scapegrace will grow careless and spoil his work, or take to his games if he be not well looked after. Did anybody thus dream of supervising Raphael and Michael Angelo to keep them to their work? No, the master artist requires no eye to urge him on. Popes and emperors came to visit the great painters in their studios but did they paint the better because these grandees gazed upon them? Certainly not; perhaps they did all the worse in the excitement or the worry of the visit. They had regard to something better than the eye of pompous personages. So the true Christian wants no eye of man to watch him.

There may be pastors and preachers who are the better for being looked after by bishops and presbyters; but fancy a bishop overseeing the work of Martin Luther and trying to quicken his zeal; or imagine a presbyter looking after Calvin to keep him sound in the faith. Oh, no; gracious minds outgrow the governance and stimulus which comes of the oversight of mortal man. God's own Spirit dwells within us, and we serve the Lord from an inward principle, which is not fed from without. There is about a real Christian a prevailing sense that God sees him, and he does not care who else may set his eye upon him; it is enough for him that God is there. He hath small respect to the eye of man, he neither courts nor dreads it. Let the good deed remain in the dark, for God sees it there, and that is enough; or let it be blazoned in the light of day to be pecked at by the censorious, for it little matters who censures since God approves. This is to be a true servant of Christ; to escape from being an eyeservant to men by becoming in the sublimest sense an eyeservant, working ever beneath the eye of God.

Wage? Is that the motive of a Christian? Yes, in the highest sense, for the greatest of the saints, such as Moses, have 'had respect unto the recompense of the reward,' and it were like despising the reward which God promises to his people if we had no respect whatever unto it. Respect unto the reward which cometh of God kills the selfishness which is always expecting a reward from men. We can postpone our reward, and we can be content, instead of receiving present praise, to be misunderstood and misrepresented: we can postpone our reward, and we can endure instead thereof to be disappointed in our work, and to labour on without success, or when the reward does come how glorious it will be! An hour with Jesus will make up for a lifetime of persecution! One smile from him will repay us a thousand times over for all disappointments and discouragements.

10

A GREAT LEADER AND GOOD SOLDIERS

What wonders men can do when they are influenced by enthusiastic love for a leader! Alexander's troops marched thousands of miles on foot, and they would have been utterly wearied had it not been for their zeal for Alexander. He led them forth conquering and to conquer. Alexander's presence was the life of their valour, the glory of their strength. If there was a very long day's march over burning sands, one thing they knew – that Alexander marched with them; if they were thirsty, they knew that he thirsted too, for when one brought a cup of water to the king, he put it aside, thirsty as he was, and said, 'Give it to the sick soldier.' Once it so happened that they were loaded with the spoil which they had taken, and each man had become rich with goodly garments and wedges of gold; then they began to travel very slowly with so much to carry, and the king feared that he should not overtake his foe. Having a large quantity of spoil which fell to his own share, he burned it all before the eyes of his soldiers, and bade them do the like, that they might pursue the enemy and win even more. 'Alexander's portion lies beyond,' cried he, and seeing the king's own spoils on fire his warriors were content to give up their gains also and share with their king. He did himself what he commanded others to do: in self-denial and hardship he was a full partaker with his followers. After this fashion our Lord and Master acts towards us. He says, 'Renounce pleasure for the good of others. Deny yourself, and take up your cross. Suffer, though you might avoid it; labour, though you might rest, when God's glory demands suffering or labour of you. Have I not set you an example?'

'Who, though he was rich yet for our sakes he became poor, that we through his poverty might be rich.' He stripped himself of all things that he might clothe us with his glory. When we heartily serve such a Leader as this, and are fired by his spirit, then murmuring, and complaining, and weariness, and fainting of heart are altogether fled: a divine passion carries us beyond ourselves.

I believe great numbers of working men – I am not going to judge them for it – always consider how little they can possibly do to earn their wages, and the question with them is not, 'How much can we give for the wage?' that used to be; but 'How little can we give? How little work can we do in the day, without being discharged for idleness?' Many men say, 'We must not do all the work today, for we shall need something to do tomorrow: our masters will not give us more than they can help, and therefore we will not give them more than we are obliged to.' This is the general spirit on both sides, and as a nation we are going to the dogs because that spirit is among us; and we shall be more and more beaten by foreign competition if this spirit is cultivated. Among Christians such a notion cannot be tolerated in the service of our Lord Jesus. It never does for a minister to say, 'If I preach three times a week it is quite as much as anybody will expect of me; therefore I shall do no more.' It will never be right for you to say, 'I am a Sabbath school teacher; if I get into the class to the minute – some of you do not do that – and if I stop just as long as the class lasts, I need not look after the boys and girls through the week: I cannot be bothered with them; I will do just as much as I am bound to do, but no more.'

In a certain country town it was reported that the grocer's wife cut a plum in two, for fear there should be a grain more than weight in the parcel, and the folks called her Mrs. Splitplum. Ah, there are many Splitplums in religion. They do not want to do more for Jesus than may be absolutely necessary. They would like to give good weight, but they would be sorry to be convicted of doing too much. Ah, when we get to feel we are doing service for our Lord Jesus Christ, we adopt a far more liberal scale. Then we do not calculate how much ointment will suffice for his feet, but we give him all that our box contains. Is this your talk, 'Here, bring the scales, this ointment cost a great deal of money, we must be economical. Watch every drachm, yea, every scruple and grain, for the nard is costly?' If this be your cool manner of calculation your offering is not worth a fig. Not so spake that daughter of love of whom we read in the gospels, for she brake the box and poured out all the contents upon her Lord. 'To what purpose is this waste?' cried Judas. It was Judas who thus spoke, and you know therefore the worth of the observation. Christ's servants delight to give so much as to be thought wasteful, for they feel that when they have in the judgment of others done extravagantly for Christ, they have but begun to show their hearts' love for his dear name. Thus the elevating power of the spirit of consecration lifts us up above the wretched parsimony of mere formality.

'Is the work good enough?' said one to his servant. The man replied, 'Sir, it is good enough for the price: and it is good enough for the man who is going to have it.' Just so, and when we 'serve' men we may perhaps rightly judge in that fashion, but when we come to serve Christ, is anything good enough for him? Could our zeal know no respite, could our prayers know no pause, could our efforts know no relaxation, could we give all we have of time, wealth, talent and opportunity, could we die a martyr's death a thousand times, would not he, the Best Beloved of our souls, deserve far more? Ah, that he would. Therefore is self-congratulation banished forever. When you have done all, you will feel that it is not worthy of the matchless merit of Jesus, and you will be humbled at the thought. Thus, while doing all for Jesus stimulates zeal, it fosters humility, a happy blending of useful effects.

The resolve to do all as unto the Lord will elevate you above that craving for recognition which is a disease with many. It is a sad fault in many Christians that they cannot do any thing unless all the world is told of it. The hen in the farmyard has laid an egg, and feels so proud of the achievement that she must cackle about it: everybody must know of that one poor egg, till all the country round resounds with the news. It is so with some professors: their work must be published, or they can do no more. 'Here have I,' said one, 'been teaching in the school for years, and nobody ever thanked me for it; I believe that some of us who do the most are the least noticed, and what a shame it is.' But if you have done your service unto the Lord you should not talk so, or we shall suspect you of having other aims. The servant of Jesus will say, 'I do not want human notice. I did it for the Master; he noticed me, and I am content. I tried to please him, and I did please him, and therefore I ask no more, for I have gained my end. I seek no praise of men, for I fear lest the breath of human praise should tarnish the pure silver of my service.'

11

Hard Work and It's Reward

Do you not think that at times our getting lax in Christian work arises from our being very low in grace? As a rule, you cannot get out of a man that which is not in him. You cannot go forth yourself to your class and do your work vigorously if you have lost inward vigour. You cannot minister before the Lord with the unction of the Holy One if that unction is not upon you. If you are not living near to God and in the power of God, then the power of God will not go forth through you to the children of your care; so that I think we should judge, when we become discontented and downhearted, that we are out of sorts spiritually. Let us say to ourselves, 'Come! my soul! What aileth thee? This faint heart is a sign that thou art out of health. Go to the great Physician, and obtain from him a tonic which shall brace thee. Come, play the man. Have none of these whims! Away with your idleness! The reaping-time will come, therefore thrust in the plough.'

Is not another reason why we become downhearted to be found in the coldness and indifference of our fellow Christians? We see others doing the Lord's work carelessly: and when we are all on fire ourselves we find them to be cold as ice: we get among people in the church who do not seem to care whether the souls of the children are saved or not, and thus we are apt to be discouraged. The idleness of others should be an argument for our being more diligent ourselves. If our Master's work is suffering at the hands of our fellowservants should we not try to do twice as much ourselves to make up for their deficiencies? Ought not the laggards to be warnings to us lest we also come into the same lukewarm condition? To argue that I ought to be a sluggard because others loiter is poor logic.

Sometimes, too – I am ashamed to mention it – I have heard of teachers becoming weary from want of being appreciated. Their work has not been sufficiently noticed by the pastor, and praised by the superintendent, and sufficient notice has not been taken of them and their class by their fellow teachers. I will not say much about this cause of faintness, because it is so small an affair that it is quite below a Christian. Appreciation! Do we expect it in this world? The Jewish nation despised and rejected their King, and even if we were as holy as the Lord Jesus we might still fail to be rightly judged and properly esteemed. What matters it? If God accepts us we need not be dismayed, though all should pass us by.

Perhaps, however, the work itself may suggest to us a little more excuse for being weary. It is hard work to sow on the highway, and amidst the thorns – hard work to be casting good seed upon the rock year after year. Well, if I had done so for many years, and was enabled by the Holy Ghost, I would say to myself: 'I shall not give up my work because I have not yet received a recompense in it, for I perceive that in the Lord's parable three sowings did not succeed, and yet the one piece of good ground paid for all. Perhaps I have gone through my three unsuccessful sowings, and now is my time to enjoy my fourth, in which the seed will fall upon good ground.' It is a pity, when you have had some years of rough work, to give all up *now*. Why, now you are going to enjoy the sweets of your former labour. It would be a pity, just when you have mastered your class, and prepared the way for a blessing, for you to run away from it. There is so much less of difficulty for you to overcome by as much as you have already overcome. He who has passed so many miles of a rough voyage will not have to go over those miles again: do not let him think of going back. To go back, indeed, in this pilgrimage were shameful: and as we have no armour for our back, it would be dangerous. Putting our hand to this plough and looking back will prove that we were unworthy of the kingdom. If there be a hundred reasons for giving up your work of faith, there are fifty thousand for going on with it. Though there are many arguments for fainting, there are far more arguments for persevering. Though we might be weary, and do sometimes feel so, let us wait upon the Lord and renew our strength, and we shall mount up with wings as eagles, forget our weariness, and be strong in the Lord and in the power of his might.

We have abundant encouragement in the prospect of reward. 'In due season we shall reap, if we faint not.'

The reaping time will come. Our chief business is to glorify God by teaching the truth whether souls are saved or not; but still I demur to the statement that we may go on preaching the gospel for years and years, and even all our lifetime, and yet no result may follow. They say, 'Paul *may* plant and Apollos *may* water, but God giveth the increase.' I should like them to find that passage in the Bible. In my English Bible it runs thus: 'I (Paul) have planted, Apollos watered; but God gave the increase.' There is not the slightest intent to teach us that when Paul planted and Apollos watered, God would arbitrarily refuse the increase. All the glory is claimed for the Lord, but honest labour is not despised. I do not say that there is the same relation between teaching the truth and conversion as there is between cause and effect, so that they are invariably connected; but I will maintain that it is the rule of the kingdom that they should be connected, through the power of the Holy Ghost. Some causes will not produce effects because certain obstacles intervene to prevent.

A person may teach the gospel in a bad spirit; that *must* spoil it. A person may teach only part of the gospel, and he may put that the wrong way upwards. God may bless it somewhat, but yet the good man may greatly retard the blessing by the mistaken manner in which he delivers the truth. Take it as a rule that the truth of God prayed over, spoken in the fear of the Lord, with the Holy Spirit dwelling in the man who speaks it, will produce the effect which is natural to it. As the rain climbs not up to the skies, and the snowflakes never take to themselves wings to rise to heaven, so neither shall the Word of God return unto him void, but it shall accomplish that which he pleases. We have not spent our strength in vain. Not a verse taught to a little girl, nor a text dropped into the ear of a careless boy, nor an earnest warning given to an obdurate young sinner, nor a loving farewell to one of the senior girls, shall be without some result or other to the glory of God. And, taking it all together as a mass, though this handful of seed may be eaten of the birds, and that other seed may die on the hard rock, yet, as a whole, the seed shall spring up in sufficient abundance to plentifully reward the sower and the giver of the seed.

We know that our labour is not in vain in the Lord. Go to your classes with this persuasion, 'I shall not labour in vain, or spend my strength for naught.' 'According to your faith, so be it unto you.' Take a little measure, and you shall have it filled with the manna of success, but take a great omer, and in its fulness you shall have abundance. Believe in the power of the truth you teach. Believe in the power of Christ about whom you speak. Believe in the omnipotence of the Holy Ghost, whose help you have invoked in earnest prayer. Go to your sowing, and reckon upon reaping.

'Let *us* not be weary, for *we* shall reap.' *We* shall reap. It is not, 'We shall do the work, and our successors shall reap after we are gone.' We ought to be very pleased even with that, and no doubt such is often the case. But *we* shall reap too. Yes, I shall have my sheaves, and you will have yours. The plot which I have toiled and wept over shall yield me my sheaves of harvest, and I shall personally gather them. I shall reap. 'I never thought much of myself as a teacher,' says one, 'I always feel that I am hardly competent, and I notice that the superintendent has only trusted me with the little children; but I am so glad to hear that I shall reap. I shall reap. I shall have a dear little one, saved in the Lord, to be my portion.' I pray you, if you have never reaped yet, begin to hope. You teachers who are always punctual, I mean: of course, if you do not come in time, you do not care whether you reap or not; but I speak to punctual teachers, I speak also to earnest teachers for if you are not earnest you will never reap: you punctual, earnest, prayerful teachers shall reap. Some teachers do not go in for reaping, and they will not enjoy it.

But I am speaking now to real, hard-working, earnest Sunday school teachers who give their hearts to it, and yet have seen no results. According to the text, you shall reap. Come, my persevering comrades, let us not be discouraged: 'In due season *we* shall reap,' even we. You shall have your share with others. Though you feel as though you must give it up, you shall yet reap.

After sowing all this while, do not cease from labour when reaping time is so near. If I were a farmer, if I did give up my farm, it should be before I sowed my wheat, but if I had done all the ploughing and the sowing, I should not say to my landlord, 'There are six weeks and then cometh harvest, and I desire to let another tenant come in.' No, no. I should want to stop and see the harvest gathered and the wheat taken to market. I should want to have my reward. So wait for your recompense, especially you that have been discouraged. 'In due time we shall reap, if we faint not.' We who have thought least of our service, and perhaps have exercised least faith, and endured most searchings of heart and most groaning and crying before the Lord, we also 'in due season shall reap, if we faint not.'

12

Workers Reading to Profit

I am afraid that this is a magazine-reading age, a newspaper-reading age, a periodical-reading age, but not so much a Bible–reading age as it ought to be. In Puritanic times men used to have a scant supply of other literature, but they found a library enough in the one Book, the Bible. And how they did read the Bible! How little of Scripture there is in modern sermons compared with the sermons of those masters of theology, the Puritanic divines! Almost every sentence of theirs seems to cast sidelights upon a text of Scripture; not only the one they are preaching about, but many others as well are set in a new light as the discourse proceeds. They introduce blended lights from other passages which are parallel or semi-parallel thereunto, and thus they educate their readers to compare spiritual things with spiritual. I would to God that we ministers kept more closely to the grand old Book!

We should be instructive preachers if we did so, even if we were ignorant of 'modern thought,' and were not 'abreast of the times.' I warrant you we should be leagues ahead of our times if we kept closely to the Word of God. As for you who have not to preach, the best food for you is the Word of God itself. Sermons and books are well enough, but streams that run for a long distance above ground gradually gather for themselves somewhat of the soil through which they flow, and they lose the cool freshness with which they started from the spring head. Truth is sweetest where it breaks from the smitten Rock, for at its first gush it has lost none of its heavenliness and vitality. It is always best to drink at the well and not from the tank. You shall find that reading the Word of God for yourselves, reading *it* rather than notes upon it, is the surest way of growing in grace. Drink of the unadulterated milk of the Word of God, and not of the skim milk, or the milk and water of man's word.

Much apparent Bible reading is not Bible reading at all. The verses pass under the eye, and the sentences glide over the mind, but there is no true reading. An old preacher used to say, the Word has mighty free course among many nowadays, for it goes in at one of their ears and out at the other; so it seems to be with some readers – they can read a very great deal, because they do not read anything. The eye glances, but the mind never rests. The soul does not light upon the truth and stay there. It flits over the landscape as a bird might do, but it builds no nest therein, and finds no rest for the sole of its foot. Such reading is not reading. Understanding the meaning is the essence of true reading. Reading has a kernel to it, and the mere shell is of little worth. In prayer there is such a thing as praying in prayer. So in praise there is a praising in song, an inward fire of intense devotion which is the life of the hallelujah. It is so in fasting; there is a fasting which is not fasting, and there is an inward fasting, a fasting of the soul, which is the soul of fasting. It is even so with the reading of the Scriptures. There is an interior reading, a kernel reading – a true and living reading of the Word. This is the soul of reading; and if it be not there, the reading is a mechanical exercise and profits nothing.

Certainly, the benefit of reading must come to the soul by the way of the understanding. When the high priest went into the holy place he always lit the golden candlestick before he kindled the incense upon the brazen altar, as if to show that the mind must have illumination before the affections can properly rise towards their divine object. There must be knowledge of God before there can be love to God: there must be a knowledge of divine things, as they are revealed, before there can be an enjoyment of them. We must try to make out, as far as our finite mind can grasp it, what God means by this and what he means by that; otherwise we may kiss the Book and have no love to its contents, we may reverence the letter and yet really have no devotion towards the Lord who speaks to us in these words. You will never get comfort to your soul out of what you do not understand, nor find guidance for your life out of what you do not comprehend, nor can any practical bearing upon your character come out of that which is not understood by you.

When we come to the study of Holy Scripture we should try to have our mind well awake to it. We are not always fit, it seems to me, to read the Bible. At times it were well for us to stop before we open the volume. 'Put off thy shoes from off thy feet, for the place whereon thou standest is holy ground.' You have just come in from careful thought and anxiety about your worldly business, and you cannot immediately take that book and enter into its heavenly mysteries. As you ask a blessing over your meat before you fall to, so it would be a good rule for you to ask a blessing on the Word before you partake of its heavenly food.

Pray the Lord to strengthen your eyes before you dare to look into the eternal light of Scripture. As the priests washed their feet at the laver before they went to their holy work, so it were well to wash the soul's eyes with which you look upon God's Word, to wash even the fingers, if I may so speak – the mental fingers with which you will turn from page to page – that with a holy book you may deal after a holy fashion. Say to your soul, 'Come, soul, wake up; thou art not now about to read the newspaper; thou art not now perusing the pages of a human poet, to be dazzled by his flashing poetry; thou art coming very near to God, who sits in the Word like a crowned monarch in his halls. Wake up, my glory; wake up all that is within me. Though just now I may not be praising and glorifying God, I am about to consider that which should lead me so to do, and therefore it is an act of devotion. So be on the stir, my soul; be on the stir, and bow not sleepily before the awful throne of the Eternal.'

Scripture reading is our spiritual mealtime. Sound the gong and call in every faculty to the Lord's own table to feast upon the precious meat which is now to be partaken of; or, rather, ring the church bell as for worship, for the studying of the Holy Scripture ought to be as solemn a deed as when we sing the hymns upon the Sabbath day in the courts of the Lord's house.

To understand what you read, you will need to meditate upon it. Some passages of Scripture lie clear before us – blessed shallows in which the lambs may wade; but there are deeps in which our mind might rather drown herself than swim with pleasure, if she came there without caution. There are texts of Scripture which are made and constructed on purpose to make us think. By this means, among others, our heavenly Father would educate us for heaven – by making us think our way into divine mysteries. Hence he puts the Word in a somewhat involved form to compel us to meditate upon it before we reach the sweetness of it. He might, you know, have explained it to us so that we might catch the thought in a minute, but he does not please to do so in every case. Many of the veils which are cast over Scripture are not meant to hide the meaning from the diligent, but to compel the mind to be active, for oftentimes the diligence of the heart in seeking to know the divine mind does the heart more good than the knowledge itself.

Meditation and careful thought exercise us and strengthen the soul for the reception of the yet more lofty truths. I have heard that the mothers in the Balearic isles, in the old times, who wanted to bring their boys up to be good slingers, would put their dinners up above them where they could not get at them until they threw a stone and fetched them down; our Lord wishes us to be good slingers, and he puts up some precious truth in a lofty place where we cannot get it down except by slinging at it; and, at last, we hit the mark and find food for our souls. Then have we the double benefit of learning the art of meditation and partaking of the sweet truth which it has brought within our reach.

We must meditate. These grapes will yield no wine till we tread upon them. These olives must be put under the wheel, and pressed again and again, that the oil may flow therefrom. In a dish of nuts, you may know which nut has been eaten, because there is a little hole which the insect has punctured through the shell – just a little hole, and then inside there is the living thing eating up the kernel. Well, it is a grand thing to bore through the shell of the letter, and then to live inside feeding upon the kernel. I would wish to be such a little worm as that, living within and upon the Word of God, having bored my way through the shell, and having reached the innermost mystery of the blessed gospel. The Word of God is always most precious to the man who most lives upon it. As I sat under a wide-spreading beech, I was pleased to mark with prying curiosity the singular habits of that most wonderful of trees, which seems to have an intelligence about it which other trees have not. I wondered and admired the beech, but I thought to myself, I do not think half as much of this beech tree as yonder squirrel does. I see him leap from bough to bough, and I feel sure that he dearly values the old beech tree, because he has his home somewhere inside it in a hollow place, these branches are his shelter, and those beechnuts are his food. He lives upon the tree. It is his world, his playground, his granary, his home; indeed, it is everything to him, and it is not so to me, for I find my rest and food elsewhere. With God's Word it is well for us to be like squirrels, living in it and living on it. Let us exercise our minds by leaping from bough to bough of it, and find our rest and food in it, and make it our all in all. There are hiding places in it; comfort and protection are there. We shall be the people that get the profit out of it if we make it to be our food, our medicine, our treasury, our armoury, our rest, our delight. May the Holy Ghost lead us to do this, and make the Word thus precious to our souls.

Use all means and helps towards the understanding of the Scriptures. When Philip asked the Ethiopian eunuch whether he understood the prophecy of Isaiah he replied, 'How can I, unless some man should guide me?' Then Philip went up and opened to him the Word of the Lord. Some, under the pretence of being taught of the Spirit of God, refuse to be instructed by books or by living men. This is no honouring of the Spirit of God; it is a disrespect to him, for if he gives to some of his servants more light than to others – and it is clear he does – then they are bound to give that light to others, and to use it for the good of the church. But if the other part of the church refuse to receive that light, to what end did the Spirit of God give it? This would imply that there is a mistake somewhere in the economy of gifts and graces, which is managed by the Holy Spirit. It cannot be so. The Lord Jesus Christ pleases to give more knowledge of his Word and more insight into it to some of his servants than to others, and it is ours joyfully to accept the knowledge which he gives in such ways as he chooses to give it. It would be most wicked of us to say, 'We will not have the heavenly treasure which exists in earthen vessels. If God will give us the heavenly treasure out of his own hand, but not through the earthen vessel, we will have it;

but we think we are too wise, too heavenly-minded, too spiritual altogether to care for jewels, when they are placed in earthen pots. We will not hear anybody, and we will not read anything except *the Book* itself, neither will we accept any light, except that which comes in through a crack in our own roof. We will not see by another man's candle, we would sooner remain in the dark.' Do not let us fall into such folly. Let the light come from God, and though a child shall bring it, we will joyfully accept it.

In reading we ought to seek out the spiritual teaching of the word. Our Lord says, ' Have ye not read?' Then, again, 'Have ye not read?' and then he says, 'If ye had known what this meaneth,' and the meaning is something very spiritual. The text he quoted was, 'I will have mercy, and not sacrifice' – a text out of the prophet Hosea. Now the scribes and Pharisees were all for the letter – the sacrifice, the killing of the bullock, and so on. They overlooked the spiritual meaning of the passage, 'I will have mercy, and not sacrifice' – namely, that God prefers that we should care for our fellow creatures rather than that we should observe any ceremonial of his law, so as to cause hunger or thirst, and thereby death, to any of the creatures that his hands have made. They ought to have passed beyond the outward into the spiritual, and all our readings ought to do the same.

This should be the case when we read the historical passages, 'Have ye not read what David

did, when he was an hungered, and they that were
with him; how he entered into the house of God,
and did eat the shewbread, which was not lawful for
him to eat, neither for them which were with him,
but only for the priests?' This was a piece of history,
and they ought so to have read it as to have found
spiritual instruction in it. I have sometimes found
even a greater depth of spirituality in the histories
than I have in the Psalms. When you reach the inner
and spiritual meaning of a history you are often
surprised at the wondrous clearness – the realistic
force – with which the teaching comes home to your
soul. Some of the most marvellous mysteries of
revelation are better understood by being set before
our eyes in the histories than they are by the verbal
declaration of them. When we have the statement to
explain the illustration, the illustration expands and
vivifies the statement. For instance, when our Lord
himself would explain to us what faith was, he sent
us to the history of the brazen serpent; and who that
has ever read the story of the brazen serpent has not
felt that he has had a better idea of faith through the
picture of the dying snake-bitten persons looking
to the serpent of brass and living, than from any
description which even Paul has given us, wondrously
as he defines and describes?

Just the same thing is true with regard to all *the
ceremonial precepts*, because the Saviour goes on to
say, 'Have ye not read in the law, how that on the

Sabbath days the priests in the temple profane the Sabbath, and are blameless?' There is not a single precept in the old law but has an inner sense and meaning; therefore do not turn away from Leviticus, or say, 'I cannot read these chapters in the Books of Exodus and Numbers. They are all about the tribes and their standards, the stations in the wilderness and the halts of the march, the tabernacle and furniture, or about golden knops and bowls, and boards, and sockets, and precious stones, and blue and scarlet and fine linen.' No, but look for the inner meaning. Make thorough search; for as in a king's treasure that which is the most closely locked up and the hardest to come at is the choicest jewel of the treasure, so is it with the Holy Scriptures.

Did you ever go to the British Museum Library? There are many books of reference there which the reader is allowed to take down when he pleases. There are other books for which he must write a ticket, and he cannot get them without the ticket; but they have certain choice books which you will not see without a special order, and then there is an unlocking of doors, and an opening of cases, and there is a watcher with you while you make your inspection. You are scarcely allowed to put your eye on the manuscript, for fear you should blot a letter out by glancing at it; it is such a precious treasure; there is not another copy of it in all the world, and so you cannot get at it easily. Just so, there are choice and precious doctrines of God's Word which are locked up in such cases as Leviticus or Solomon's Song, and you cannot get at them without a deal of unlocking of doors; and the Holy Spirit himself must be with you, or else you will never come at the priceless treasure. The higher truths are as choicely hidden away as the precious regalia of princes; therefore *search* as well as read. Do not be satisfied with a ceremonial precept till you reach its spiritual meaning, for that is true reading. You have not read till you understand the spirit of the matter.

You will get a thousand helps out of that wondrous book if you do but read it; for, understanding the words more, you will prize it more, and, as you get older, the Book will grow with your growth, and turn out to be a greybeard's manual of devotion just as it was aforetime a child's sweet story book. Yes, it will always be a new book – just as new a Bible as if it was printed yesterday, and nobody had ever seen a word of it till now; and yet it will be a deal more precious for all the memories which cluster round it. As we turn over its pages how sweetly do we recollect passages in our history which will never be forgotten to all eternity, but will stand forever intertwined with gracious promises. The Lord teach us to read his book of life which he has opened before us here below, so that we may read our titles clear in that other book of love which we have not seen as yet, but which will be opened at the last great day.

13

Save the Children

I hope you do not altogether forget the Sabbath school, and yet I am afraid a great many Christians are scarcely aware that there are such things as Sabbath schools at all; they know it by hearsay, but not by observation. Probably in the course of twenty years they have never visited the school or concerned themselves about it. They would be gratified to hear of any success accomplished, but though they may not have heard anything about the matter one way or the other, they are well content. In most churches you will find a band of young and ardent spirits giving themselves to Sunday school work; but there are numbers of others who might greatly strengthen the school who never attempt anything of the sort. In this they might be excused if they had other work to do; but, unfortunately, they have no godly occupation, but are mere killers of time, while this work which lies ready to hand, and is accessible, and demands their assistance, is entirely neglected. I will not say there are any such sluggards here, but I am not able to believe that we are quite free from them, and therefore I will ask conscience to do its work with the guilty parties.

Children need to be saved; children may be saved; children are to be saved by instrumentality. Children may be saved while they are children. He who said, 'Suffer the little children to come unto me, and forbid them not, for of such is the kingdom of heaven,' never intended that his church should say, 'We will look after the children by and by when they have grown up to be young men and women.' He intended that it should be a subject of prayer, and earnest endeavour that children as children should be converted to God. The conversion of a child involves the same work of divine grace, and results in the same blessed consequences as the conversion of the adult. There is the saving of the soul from death in the child's case, and the hiding of a multitude of sins, but there is this additional matter for joy, that a great preventive work is done when the young are converted. Conversion saves a child from a multitude of sins. If God's eternal mercy shall bless your teaching to a little prattler, how happy that boy's life will be compared with what might have been if it had grown up in folly, sin and shame, and had only been converted after many days! It is the highest wisdom and the truest prudence for our children that while they are yet young their hearts may be given to the Saviour. To reclaim the prodigal is well, but to save from ever being a prodigal is better. To bring back the thief and the drunkard is a praiseworthy action, but so to act that the boy shall never become a thief nor a drunkard is far better: hence Sabbath school instruction stands very high in the lists of philanthropic enterprises, and Christians ought to be most earnest in it. He who converts a child from the error of his way prevents as well as covers a multitude of sins.

And, moreover, it gives the church the hope of being furnished with the best of men and women. The church's Samuels and Solomons are made wise in their youth; Davids and Josiahs were tender of heart when they were tender in years. Read the lives of the most eminent ministers and you shall usually find that their Christian history began early. Though it is not absolutely needful, yet it is highly propitious to the growth of a well developed Christian character, that its foundation should be laid on the basis of youthful piety. I do not expect to see the churches of Jesus Christ ordinarily built up by those who have through life lived in sin, but by the bringing up in their midst, in the fear and admonition of the Lord, young men and women who become pillars in the house of our God. If we want strong Christians we must look to those who were Christians in their youth; trees must be planted in the courts of the Lord while yet young if they are to flourish well and long.

The Spirit of God waits to help us in this effort. He is with us if we be with him. He is ready to bless the humblest teacher, and even the infant classes shall not be without a benediction. He can give us words and thoughts suitable to our little auditory. He can so bless us that we shall know how to speak a word in season to the youthful ear. And oh, if it be not so, if teachers are not found, or, being found, are unfaithful, we shall see the children that have been in our schools go back into the world like their parents, hating religion because of the tedium of hours spent in the Sunday school, and we shall produce a race of infidels, or a generation of superstitious persons; the golden opportunity will be lost, and most solemn responsibility will rest upon us. I pray the church of God to think much of the Sunday school. I beseech all lovers of the nation to pray for Sunday schools; I entreat all who love Jesus Christ and would see his kingdom come, to be very tender towards all youthful people, and to pray that their hearts may be won to Jesus.

The theme lies very near my heart. It is one which ought to press heavily upon all our consciences. God must lead your thoughts fully into it; I leave it, but not till I have asked these questions: What have you been doing for the conversion of children, each one of you? What have you done for the conversion of your own children? Are you quite clear upon that matter? Do you ever put your arms around your boy's neck and pray for him and with him? Father, you will find that such an act will exercise great influence over your lad.

Mother, do you ever talk to your little daughter about Christ, and him crucified? Under God's hands you may be a spiritual as well as a natural mother to that well-beloved child of yours. What are you doing, you who are guardians and teachers of youth? Are you clear about their souls? You, weekday schoolmasters, as well as you who labour on the Sabbath, are you doing all you should that your boys and girls may be brought early to confess the Lord? I leave it with yourselves. You shall receive a great reward if, when you enter heaven, as I trust you will, you shall find many dear children there to welcome you into eternal habitations; it will add another heaven to your own heaven, to meet with heavenly beings who shall salute you as their teacher who brought them to Jesus. I would not wish to go to heaven alone – would you? I would not wish to have a crown in heaven without a star in it, because no soul was ever saved by my means – would you?

There they go, the sacred flock of blood-bought sheep, the great Shepherd leads them; many of them are followed by twins, and others have each one their lamb; would you like to be a barren sheep of the great Shepherd's flock? The scene changes. Hearken to the trampings of a great host. I hear their war music, my ears are filled with their songs of victory. The warriors are coming home and each one is bringing his trophy on his shoulder, to the honour of the great Captain. They stream through the gate of pearl, they march in triumph to the celestial Capitol, along the golden streets, and each soldier bears with him his own portion of the spoil. Will you be there? And being there will you march without a trophy, and add nothing to the pomp of the triumph? Will you bear nothing that you have won in battle, nothing which you have ever taken for Jesus with your sword and with your bow?

Again, another scene is before me: I hear them shout the 'harvest home,' and see the reapers bearing every one his sheaf. Some of them are bowed down with the heaps of sheaves which load the happy shoulders: these went forth weeping, but they have come again rejoicing, bringing the sheaves with them. Yonder comes one who bears but a little handful, but it is rich grain; he had but a tiny plot and a little seed corn entrusted to him, and it has multiplied well according to the rule of proportion. Will you be there without so much as a solitary ear; never having ploughed nor sown, and therefore never having reaped? If so, every shout of every reaper might well strike a fresh pang into your heart as you remember that you did not sow and therefore could not reap. If you do not love my Master, do not profess to do so. If he never bought you with his blood, do not lie unto him, and come unto his table, and say that you are his servant; but if his dear wounds bought you, give yourself to him; and if you love him, feed his sheep and feed his lambs. He stands here unseen by my sight, but recognized by my faith; he exhibits to you the marks of the wounds upon his hands and his feet, and he says to you, Peace be unto you! As my Father hath sent me even so send I you. Go ye into all the world and preach the gospel to every creature; and this know, that he that converteth a sinner from the error of his ways shall save a soul from death, and shall hide a multitude of sins.

[James 5:10]

If any one of you has been the victim of violence
he is the best, well it said that this violence. The pass and truth of it, he sure of it, or consolidated by it.
Distinguished by it of him, kneel at good news sketch
it. To non-knowing soon to be a you, carry may you
heart of them, possible impress in the nobility of it.
Save the fact know, do not say in, any audience of
saying, and more extant, right of it at right a the
path. What is it that you understand? These very that
he be absent in distance from the sorry. It's when
shall we a manifest death. Then these energy were
knowing arm as shall mutual. This we are with
seeming of which we not more even fear as between
even upon them, for they have more gave, more possess
hope they have charged the look of at the have knee,
not good to you rives to resist the down side, they
he when more to make their own case, until not any
honors that they might arm with their right prison the

14

'Saving a Soul From Death'
(James 5:20)

If any one of you has been the means of bringing back a backslider, it is said, 'Let him know.' That is, let him think of it, be sure of it, be comforted by it, be inspirited by it. 'Let him know' it, and never doubt it. Do not merely hear it, let it sink deep into your heart. When an apostle inspired of the Holy Ghost says, 'Let him know,' do not let any indolence of spirit forbid your ascertaining the full weight of the truth. What is it that you are to know? To know that he who converteth a sinner from the error of his ways shall save a soul from death. This is something worth knowing, it is no small matter. Why, we have men among us whom we honour every time we cast our eyes upon them, for they have saved many precious lives; they have manned the lifeboat or they have plunged into the river to rescue the drowning; they have been ready to risk their own lives amid burning timbers that they might snatch the perishing from the devouring flames. True heroes these, far worthier of renown than your bloodstained men of war. God bless the brave hearts! May England never lack a body of worthy men to make her shores illustrious for humanity.

When we see a fellow creature exposed to danger our pulse beats quickly, and we are agitated with desire to save him. Is it not so? But the saving of a soul from death is a far greater matter. Let us think what that death is! It is not non-existence; I do not know that I would lift a finger to save my fellow creature from mere non-existence. I see no great hurt in annihilation; certainly nothing that would alarm me as a punishment for sin. Just as I see no great joy in mere eternal existence, if that is all that is meant by eternal life, so I discern no terror in ceasing to be; I would as soon not be as be, so far as mere colourless being or not being is concerned. But eternal life in Scripture means a very different thing to eternal existence; it means existing with all the faculties developed in fulness of joy; existing not as the dried herb in the hay, but as the flower in all its beauty. To die in Scripture, and indeed in common language, is not to cease to exist. Very wide is the difference between the two words to die and to be annihilated. To die as to the first death is the separation of the body from the soul; it is the resolution of our nature into its component elements; and to die the second death is to separate the man, soul and body, from his God, who is the life and joy of our manhood. This is eternal destruction from the presence of the Lord and from the glory of his power; this is to have the palace of manhood destroyed and turned into a desolate ruin for the howling dragon of remorse and the hooting owl of despair to inherit forever.

Now, remember your Saviour came to this world with two objects: he came to destroy death and to put away sin. If you convert a sinner from the error of his ways, you are made like to him in both these works: after your manner in the power of the Spirit of God you overcome death, by snatching a soul from the second death, and you also put away sin from the sight of God by hiding a multitude of sins beneath the propitiation of the Lord Jesus.

The apostle does not say if you convert a sinner from the error of his ways you will have honour. True philanthropy scorns such a motive. He does not say if you convert a sinner from the error of his ways you will have the respect of the church and the love of the individual. Such will be the case, but we are moved by far nobler motives. The joy of doing good is found in the good itself: the reward of a deed of love is found in its own result. If we have saved a soul from death, and hidden a multitude of sins, that is payment enough, though no ear should ever hear of the deed, and no pen should ever record it. Let it be forgotten that we were the instrument if good be but effected; it shall give us joy even if we be not appreciated and are left in the cold shade of forgetfulness. Yea, if others wear the honours of the good deed which the Lord has wrought by us we will not murmur; it shall be joy enough to know that a soul has been saved from death, and a multitude of sins have been covered.

Let us recollect that the saving of souls from death honours Jesus, for there is no saving souls except through his blood. As for you and for me, what can we do in saving a soul from death? Of ourselves nothing, any more than that pen which lies upon the table could write the *Pilgrim's Progress*; yet let a Bunyan grasp the pen, and the matchless work is written. So you and I can do nothing to convert souls till God's eternal Spirit takes us in hand but then he can do wonders by us, and get to himself glory by us, while it shall be joy enough to us to know that Jesus is honoured, and the Spirit magnified. Nobody talks of Homer's pen, no one has encased it in gold, or published its illustrious achievements; nor do we wish for honour among men: it will be enough for us to have been the pen in the Saviour's hand with which he has written the covenant of his grace upon the fleshy tablets of human hearts. This is golden wages for a man who really loves his Master; Jesus is glorified, sinners are saved.

All that is said by the apostle is about the conversion of one person. 'If any of you do err from the truth, and one convert *him,* let him know that he who converteth *the sinner* from the error of his ways shall save a *soul* from death.' Have you never wished you were a Whitefield? Have you never felt, in your inmost soul, great aspirations to be another McCheyne, or Brainerd, or Moffat? Cultivate the aspiration, but at the same time be happy to bring one sinner to Jesus Christ, for he who converts one is bidden to know that no mean thing is done; he has saved a soul from death, and covered a multitude of sins.

And it does not say anything about the person who is the means of this work. It is not said, 'If a minister shall convert a man, or if some noted eloquent divine shall have wrought it.' If this deed shall be performed by the least babe in our Israel, if a little child shall tell the tale of Jesus to its father, if a servant girl shall drop a tract where some one poor soul shall find it and receive salvation, if the humblest preacher at the street corner shall have spoken to the thief or to the harlot, and such shall be saved, let him know that he that turneth any sinner from the error of his ways, whoever he may be, hath saved a soul from death, and covered a multitude of sins.

Let us long to be used in the conversion of sinners. James does not speak concerning the Holy Ghost in this passage, nor of the Lord Jesus Christ, for he was writing to those who would not fail to remember the important truths which concern both the Spirit and the Son of God; but yet we cannot do spiritual good to our fellow creatures apart from the Spirit of God, neither can we be blessed to them if we do not preach to them 'Jesus Christ and him crucified.' God must use us; let us pray and pine to be used; let us purge ourselves of everything that would prevent our being employed by the Lord. If there is anything we are doing, or leaving undone, any evil we are harbouring, or any grace we are neglecting, which may make us unfit to be used of God, let us pray the Lord to cleanse, and mend, and scour us till we are vessels fit for the Master's use. Then let us be on the watch for opportunities of usefulness; let us go about the world with our ears and our eyes open, ready to avail ourselves of every occasion for doing good; let us not be content till we are useful, but make this the main design and ambition of our lives.

15

RESTORING THOSE WHO HAVE ERRED

James is pre-eminently practical. If he were, indeed, the James who was called the Just, I can understand how he earned the title, for that distinguishing trait in his character shows itself in his Epistle; and if he were 'the Lord's brother,' he did well to show so close a resemblance to his great relative and Master, who commenced his ministry with the practical Sermon on the Mount. We ought to be very grateful that in the Holy Scriptures we have food for all classes of believers, and employment for all the faculties of the saints. It was meet that the contemplative should be furnished with abundant subjects for thought – Paul has supplied them; he has given to us sound doctrine, arranged in the symmetry of exact order; he has given us deep thoughts and profound teachings; he has opened up the deep things of God.

No man who is inclined to reflection and thoughtfulness will be without food so long as the Epistles of Paul are extant, for he feeds the soul with sacred manna. For those whose predominating affections and imagination incline them to more mystic themes, John has written sentences aglow with devotion and blazing with love. We have his simple but sublime Epistles – epistles which, when you glance at them, seem in their wording to be fit for children, but when examined, their sense is seen to be too sublime to be fully grasped by the most advanced of men. You have from that same eagle-eyed and eagle-winged apostle the wondrous vision of the Revelation, where awe, devotion and imagin-ation may enlarge their flight and find scope for the fullest exercise. There will always be, however, a class of persons who are more practical than contemplative, more active than imaginative, and it was wise that there should be a James, whose main point should be to stir up their pure minds by way of remembrance, and help them to persevere in the practical graces of the Holy Spirit.

Here is a special case of a backslider from the visible church: 'if any of you' must refer to a professed Christian. The erring one had been named by the name of Jesus, and for a while had followed the truth; but in an evil hour he had been betrayed into doctrinal error, and had erred from the truth. It was not merely that he fell into a mistake upon some lesser matter which might be compared to the fringe of the gospel, but he erred in some vital doctrine – he departed from the faith in its fundamentals. There are some truths which must be believed, they are essential to salvation, and if not heartily accepted the soul will be ruined. This man had been professedly orthodox, but he turned aside from the truth on an essential point. Now, in those days the saints did not say: 'We must be largely charitable, and leave this brother to his own opinion; he sees truth from a different stand point, and has a rather different way of putting it, but his opinions are as good as our own, and we must not say that he is in error.' That is at present the fashionable way of trifling with divine truth and making things pleasant all round. Thus the gospel is debased and another gospel propagated. O God, deliver us from this deceitful infidelity, which while it does damage to the erring man, and often prevents his being reclaimed, does yet more mischief to our own hearts by teaching us that truth is unimportant, and falsehood a trifle, and so destroys our allegiance to the God of truth, and makes us traitors instead of loyal subjects to the King of kings.

It appears that this man, having erred from the truth, followed the natural logical conse-quence of doctrinal error and erred in his life as well; for the twentieth verse, which must of course be read in connection with the nineteenth, speaks of him as a 'sinner converted from the error of his way.' His way went wrong after his thought had gone wrong. You cannot deviate from truth without ere long, in some measure, at any rate, deviating from practical righteousness. This man had erred from right acting because he had erred from right believing. Suppose a man shall imbibe a doctrine which leads him to think little of Christ, he will soon have little faith in him, and become little obedient to him, and so will wander into self-righteousness or licentiousness. Let him think lightly of the punishment of sin, it is natural that he will commit sin with less compunction and burst through all restraints. Let him deny the need of atonement, and the same result will follow if he acts out his belief. Every error has its own outgrowth, as all decay has its appropriate fungus. It is in vain for us to imagine that holiness will be as readily produced from erroneous as from truthful doctrine. Do men gather grapes of thorns, or figs of thistles? The facts of history prove the contrary. When truth is dominant morality and holiness are abundant; but when error comes to the front godly living retreats in shame.

The point aimed at with regard to this sinner in thought and deed was his conversion – the turning of him round, the bringing him to right thinking and to right acting. Alas! I fear many do not look upon backsliders in this light, neither do they regard them as hopeful subjects for conversion. I have known a person who has erred, hunted down like a wolf. He was wrong to some degree, but that wrong had been aggravated and dwelt upon till the man has been worried into defiance; the fault has been exaggerated into a double wrong by ferocious attacks upon it.

The manhood of the man has taken sides with his error because he has been so severely handled. The man has been compelled, sinfully I admit, to take up an extreme position, and to go further into mischief, because he could not brook to be denounced instead of being reasoned with. And when a man has been blameworthy in his life it will often happen that his fault has been blazed abroad, retailed from mouth to mouth, and magnified, until the poor erring one has felt degraded, and having lost all self-respect has given way to far more dreadful sins. The object of some professors seems to be to amputate the limb rather than to heal it. Justice has reigned instead of mercy. Away with him! He is too foul to be washed, too diseased to be restored. This is not according to the mind of Christ, nor after the model of apostolic churches.

In the days of James, if any erred from the truth and from holiness, there were brethren found who sought their recovery, and whose joy it was thus to save a soul from death, and to hide a multitude of sins. There is something very significant in that expression, 'Brethren, if any *of you* do err from the truth.' It is akin to that other word, 'Considering thyself also, lest thou also be tempted,' and that other exhortation, 'Let him that thinketh he standeth take heed lest he fall.' He who has erred was one of yourselves, one who sat with you at the communion table, one with whom you took sweet counsel; he has been deceived, and by the subtlety of Satan he has been decoyed, but do not judge him harshly, above all do not leave him to perish unpitied.

If he ever was a saved man, he is your brother still, and it should be your business to bring back the prodigal and so to make glad your Father's heart. 'Still for all slips of his,' he is one of God's children, follow him up and do not rest till you lead him home again. And if he be not a child of God, if his professed conversion was a mistake, or a pretence, if he only made a profession, but had not the possession of vital godliness, yet still follow him with sacred importunity of love, remembering how terrible will be his doom for daring to play the hypocrite, and profane holy things with his unhallowed hands.

Weep over him the more if you feel compelled to suspect that he has been a wilful deceiver, for there is sevenfold cause for weeping. If you cannot resist the feeling that he never was sincere, but crept into the church under cover of a false profession, I say sorrow over him the more, for his doom must be the more terrible, and 'If any of you do err from the truth, and one convert him.' One what? One minister? No, any one among the brethren.

If the minister shall be the means of the restoration of a backslider, he is a happy man, and a good deed has been done; but there is nothing said here concerning preachers or pastors, not even a hint is given – it is left open to any one member of the church; and the plain inference, I think, is this – that every church member seeing his brother err from the truth, or err in practice, should set himself, in the power of the Holy Spirit, to this business of converting this special sinner from the error of his way.

Look after strangers by all means, but neglect not your brethren. It is the business, not of certain officers appointed by the vote of the church thereunto, but of every member of the body of Jesus Christ, to seek the good of all the other members. Still there are certain members upon whom in any one case this may be more imperative. For instance, in the case of a young believer, his father and his mother, if they be believers, are called upon by a sevenfold obligation to seek the conversion of their backsliding child.

In the case of a husband, none should be so earnest for his restoration as his wife, and the same rule holds good with regard to the wife. So also if the connection be that of friendship, he with whom you have had the most acquaintance should lie nearest to your heart, and when you perceive that he has gone aside, you should, above all others, act the shepherd towards him with kindly zeal. You are bound to do this to all your fellow Christians, but doubly bound to do it to those over whom you possess an influence, which has been gained by former intimacy, by relationship, or by any other means.

I beseech you, therefore, watch over one another in the Lord, and when ye see a brother overtaken in a fault, 'ye which are spiritual, restore such an one in the spirit of meekness.' Ye see your duty, do not neglect it.

It ought to cheer us to know that the attempt to convert a man who has erred from the truth is a hopeful one, it is one in which success may be looked for, and when the success comes it will be of the most joyful character. Verily it is a great joy to capture the wild, wandering sinner, but the joy of joys is to find the lost sheep which was once really in the fold and has sadly gone astray. It is a great thing to transmute a piece of brass into silver, but to the poor woman it was joy enough to find the piece of silver which was silver already, and had the king's stamp on it, though for a while it was lost.

To bring in a stranger and an alien, and to adopt him as a son, suggests a festival; but the most joyous feasting and the loudest music are for the son who was always a son, but had played the prodigal, and yet after being lost was found, and after being dead was made alive again. I say, ring the bells twice for the reclaimed backslider; ring them till the steeple rocks and reels. Rejoice doubly over that which had gone astray and was ready to perish, but has now been restored. John was glad when he found poor backsliding but weeping Peter, who had denied his Master and cheered and comforted him, and consorted with him, till the Lord himself had said, 'Simon, son of Jonas, lovest thou me?'

It may not appear so brilliant a thing to bring back a backslider as to reclaim a harlot or a drunkard, but in the sight of God it is no small miracle of grace, and to the instrument who has performed it it shall yield no small comfort. Seek ye, then, those who were of us but have gone from us; seek ye those who linger still in the congregation but have disgraced the church, and are put away from us, and rightly so, because we cannot countenance their uncleanness; seek them with prayers, and tears, and entreaties, if peradventure God may grant them repentance that they may be saved.

Around the Wicket Gate

Help for those who only know about Christ

C. H. Spurgeon

The greatest of all tragedies must be that of the person who dies just outside the gate of life. They are standing, as it were, just outside the Wicket gate to the church grounds – seeing the beauty of the building, knowing the people going in – but not stepping over the threshold themselves.

Almost saved but altogether lost.

This is a book of immeasurable value to those who have some knowledge of the Christian Faith but who are resisting God's call to commit their lives to him. No Christian should be without a copy, to either lend or give away to a friend or acquaintance who may be lingering at the gate.

Around the Wicket Gate is written in Spurgeon's unique style - sharp, penetrating, and easily readable. One of the most quoted preachers of modern times, his sermons have proved to be a blessing to millions. For someone thinking about Christianity, who has yet to accept Christ as their saviour, reading this book could be the most important step they ever take.

ISBN 0-90673-154-2

ONLY A
PRAYER
MEETING

——————

C.H. Spurgeon

C. H. SPURGEON
CLASSICS

"Only a Prayer Meeting"

Studies on prayer meetings and prayer meeting addresses

C. H. Spurgeon

How can we stir the church to pray?

Spurgeon considered the prayer meeting to be the heartbeat of the church and so paid particular attention to what he spoke about there.

Spurgeon used to address his church at midweek prayer meetings as well as with powerful sermons on Sundays. These addresses were generally more informal in tone and were designed to supply motivation for the church to pray. They are classic Spurgeon in a shorter format.

This volume is divided into 4 sections

Section 1 – Addresses on prayer and prayer meetings
Section 2 – Expositions of scripture
Section 3 – Incidents and illustrations
Section 4 – Addresses on practical matters in the church

Together this collection is charming, challenging and cheering! If you wanted to find out how Spurgeon fuelled his church for everyday Christian living and a life of prayer then there is no better starting place.

ISBN 1-85792-505-X

The Saint and his Saviour

The work of the Spirit in the life of the Christian

C. H. Spurgeon

This is the story of two friends on the journey of life.

One is the mentor to the other - a guide, a counsellor, but also a taskmaster and a judge. The other is a member of his family, loved despite their flaws.

In *The Saint and His Saviour*, Spurgeon takes us through the whole process of the work of the Spirit in a believer's life, from his first experience of the Lord, through the, often tumultuous, process of conversion, to the deepening knowledge of the presence of the Saviour with his people.

Captivating and challenging, Spurgeon examines how sin affects our relationship to Christ, and how we can cultivate a friendship with our Saviour.

Renowned for his love for people and his passion for the salvation of the lost, Spurgeon lays down a challenge to the unbeliever at every point. Extremely practical, *The Saint and his Saviour* also offers a hugely encouraging reminder to Christians that during the twists and turns of our spiritual walk the Lord is with us every step of the way.

ISBN 1-87167-601-0

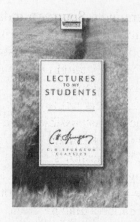

Lectures to my Students

C. H Spurgeon

Preachers often quote Spurgeon today because he had an ability to explain Christian truth to ordinary people with pointed, memorable statements. His people were effectively taught theology and enjoyed it. Spurgeon also had a sensitive and loving nature. It was this that spurred him to preach the gospel, so that as many people as possible could hear the good news about why Jesus Christ came to build a church for eternity. This passion showed through in his warm pastoring of his congregation and the setting up of a college for future ministers of the gospel.

Spurgeon realised that he could influence the church beyond his own lifetime if he could encourage future pastors to trust the Bible, love people and preach the truth fearlessly. So he collected his lectures to his college students and published this book.

If you need help in developing a love for your congregation, or need to spruce up the tools and abilities God has given you, then *Lectures to my Students* is a brilliant starting point.

ISBN 1-85792-417-7

Christ's Glorious Achievements

What Jesus has done for you

C. H Spurgeon

The popular view of Christianity today is a list of rules. Do's and Don't seems to be what it is all about. But if that's what we think Christianity is all about then we have a lot to learn. The key to understanding Christianity is not something we have to do, but rather something that Jesus Christ has already achieved on our behalf. This book, by one of the most influential Christians of the last 200 years looks at what Christ has done for us. Read it and then ask yourself the question "If Christ has done all this for me, is anything I am asked to do for Christ too much in return?"

C.H. Spurgeon preached at London's Metropolitan Tabernacle in the latter half of the nineteenth century. His books have been reprinted hundreds of times and countless thousands today find his style sharp, witty and easily readable. He is one of the most quoted preachers of modern times and his sermons have proved to be a blessing to millions.

ISBN 1-87167-628-2

Christian Focus Publications

publishes books for all ages. Our mission statement –

STAYING FAITHFUL

In dependence upon God we seek to help make his infallible word, the Bible, relevant. Our aim is to ensure that the Lord Jesus Christ is presented as the only hope to obtain forgiveness of sin, live a useful life and look forward to heaven with him.

REACHING OUT

Christ's last command requires us to reach out to our world with his gospel. We seek to help fulfill that by publishing books that point people towards Jesus and help them to develop a Christ-like maturity. We aim to equip all levels of readers for life, work ministry and mission.

Books in our adult range are published in three imprints.

Christian Focus contains popular works including biographies, commentaries, basic doctrine, and Christian living. Our children's books are also published in this imprint.

Mentor focuses on books written at a level suitable for Bible College and seminary students, pastors, and other serious readers; the imprint includes commentaries, doctrinal studies, examination of current issues, and church history.

Christian Heritage contains classic writings from the past.

Christian Focus Publications Ltd
Geanies House, Fearn, Ross-shire,
IV20 1TW, Scotland, United Kingdom
info@christianfocus.com
www.christianfocus.com